The Man Who Sold Alaska
A short biography of Alexander II, Tsar of Russia

Celebrating Alaska's Sesquicentennial–
150 years as part of the U.S. (1867 - 2017)

By Michael Dunham

mike Dunham

To: Ruth Ann Bledsoe

Library of Congress Control Number: 2016961649

ISBN: 978-1-57833-659-3

First Printing: January, 2017

Editor: Flip Todd, 𝕿𝖔𝖉𝖉 𝕮𝖔𝖒𝖒𝖚𝖓𝖎𝖈𝖆𝖙𝖎𝖔𝖓𝖘
Book Design: Vered R. Mares, 𝕿𝖔𝖉𝖉 𝕮𝖔𝖒𝖒𝖚𝖓𝖎𝖈𝖆𝖙𝖎𝖔𝖓𝖘

Printed in the United States
through Alaska Print Brokers, Anchorage, Alaska

Published by:
𝕿𝖔𝖉𝖉 𝕮𝖔𝖒𝖒𝖚𝖓𝖎𝖈𝖆𝖙𝖎𝖔𝖓𝖘
611 E. 12th Ave.
Anchorage, Alaska 99501-4603
(907) 274-TODD (8633)
Fax: (907) 929-5550
sales@toddcom.com • WWW.ALASKABOOKSANDCALENDARS.COM
with other offices in Juneau and Fairbanks, Alaska

Acknowledgments

The author wishes to thank the staffs of the University of Rochester River Campus Rush Rhees Library, the Seward House Museum in Auburn, New York and the Jilkaat Kwaan Heritage Center in Klukwan, Alaska for access to original documents and items pertaining to the transfer of Alaska from Russia to the United States. In addition to the sources listed in the bibliography, important information and insights were shared in personal communications with Herbert Hope, Grand President of the Alaska Native Brotherhood, prior to his death in 1999. A career official with the Bureau of Indian Affairs, he was an assiduous historian who collected oral histories from members of his family, Tlingits of Sitka, whose memories reached back to the Russian era.

This book is part of a two book set:
The Man Who Sold Alaska
Tsar Alexander II of Russia

&

The Man Who Bought Alaska
William H. Seward

Contents

The Man Who Sold Alaska

A short biography of Alexander II, Tsar of Russia

By Michael Dunham

One: Startling News

In March of 1867 newspaper readers in St. Petersburg, Moscow, Novgorod and Kiev learned that Tsar Alexander II, Emperor and Autocrat of All the Russias, had sold Russian America — the region now known as Alaska — to the United States.

The news hit like a gut punch. The idea was almost incomprehensible. Russia had always been obsessed with acquiring ever more territory, forging a commonwealth of various languages, races and religions that stretched 6,000 miles from Poland to the upper reaches of the Yukon River.

The Russian Empire was among the largest states in human history. From time to time a small piece might be lost to war or diplomacy. But such losses were mere temporary bad luck, the result of treacherous non-Russians, or perhaps punishment from God. They would be reclaimed sooner or later.

But this was different. A half-million square miles of Holy Russia had been given up not as a result of coercion or conflict, but for money. Without a shot.

Battles could be reversed. Treaties could be abrogated. But a commercial transaction, freely agreed to by all sides, was a solemn deal. Everyone understood that the vast colony was gone for good.

What was the Tsar thinking? Was he mad?

Alaska was a late addition to the Empire. The first explorers reached it in 1741. Fur hunters followed. By the early 1800s the colony's capital, New Archangel, was the largest European settlement on the West Coast of North America. Russians built a viable settlement in California and a briefly-occupied fort in Hawaii.

But by the mid-1800s the market for furs had collapsed. The colony was reduced to exporting ice to sweltering miners in the new boom town to the south, San Francisco. In St. Petersburg, prominent members of the ruling class questioned the profitability of the

Russian-American Company, a hybrid of government and private enterprise that held commercial rights to the colony. They accused agents of the far-off outpost of mismanagement, malfeasance and inhumane treatment of the indigenous people.

Yet a delegation sent to investigate the situation in 1860 concluded that the company was well-run, generating a reasonable return on investment and capable of much more. The land was full of natural resources: furs, coal, timber, fish. There were even rumors of gold.

Those who considered things from a global perspective knew the territory had numerous good ports near the "Great Circle Route," the shortest distance for shipping between Asia and America. With American settlers flooding into California and Oregon, industry and business were sure to follow. As steam replaced sail, the difficulties of navigating the stormy North Pacific would be conquered. Alaska occupied an excellent position for both international trade and military advantage.

Could the Tsar not see this? Was he blind?

Russians felt a blow to national pride brought on by the loss of the colony. In the first half of the 19th century most European powers had been driven from the New World. Spain, France and the Netherlands could claim only tiny remnants of their once vast holdings in the Western Hemisphere. Only two Old World countries still maintained significant possessions. Britain had Canada. And Russia owned Alaska.

The banner of the double eagle flew over New Archangel, a symbol of Russian power and dignity, a testament to Russia's rightful place among the great nations of the Earth.

Did the Tsar have no honor? No sense of patriotism?

Finally, there was the price. Russia had let all of this go — land, forts, merchandise, property, resources and opportunity — for a paltry $7.2 million. An insult. If the country really needed the money, the royal family had many times that amount in their personal bank accounts.

Was the Tsar a fool?

A modern observer looking back on the reign of Alexander II from the perspective of 150 years later may reasonably conclude that he made many mistakes.

But he was not a fool. He was not blind and he was not mad. He was among the more intelligent and perhaps the single most humane and honorable of the absolute despots who wore the imperial crown.

And he was as proud of his country as any Russian then or now.

He had reasons for selling his North American colony to an upstart democracy. They were complex reasons, as one might expect from a man known by so many different names: Warrior, Lover, Despot, Exterminator, Emancipator and Liberator.

The purpose of this book is to present a portrait of the man who sold Alaska, to examine why he did it and to put the sale into perspective with the other events of his reign.

They are monumental events. Alexander lived a life of heroic military victories, ground-breaking social reform and a sweeping romance that has supplied the story for at least two big screen movies.

But it was also a life of crushing defeats, massive human suffering, humiliation, scandal and actions that some say made inevitable the horrors of the 20th century.

And yet Russian historian Edvard Radzinsky asserts, the sale of Alaska is the one act for which Russia has still not forgiven Alexander II.

Two: A Dangerous Destiny

The successors of Tsar Michael Romanov (1596-1645) were born into a perilous life. Peter the Great (1672-1725) executed his heir, Alexei. Peter's daughter Elizabeth (1709-1761) usurped the throne from the infant Tsar Ivan VI, who spent the rest of his short, miserable life in a jail cell before being murdered.

Elizabeth's nephew Peter III (1728-1762) was killed by his wife, Catherine the Great (1726-1796), in a palace coup. Catherine's son Paul (1754-1891) was slain in a scheme that involved his own son, Alexander I (1777-1825).

The sword of Damocles dangled over the head of all Romanov rulers and their children, but the imperial family lived in luxury and enjoyed totalitarian power that astounded the rest of Europe.

Peter the Great created a military leviathan and built the largest navy in the world. He pushed his borders from the Black Sea on the south to the Baltic Sea in the north. On the shores of the Baltic he decreed the construction of a new capital, St. Petersburg, and it was done. The glorious city of palaces, canals and parade grounds rose almost overnight, erected on the bones of tens of thousands of workers who died building it.

Peter ordered Vitus Bering, a Danish sea captain in his service, to march thousands of miles to the Pacific Ocean, build ships and sail east. Bering accomplished the impossible because the Tsar's command never went unfulfilled, regardless of the cost or suffering. Bering succeeded in mapping Russia's northeast coast in 1725, including Little Diomede Island, now part of the state of Alaska.

In 1732 a crew led by Mikhail Gvozdev spotted the cape west of present-day Nome. They were looking at the edge of the Americas but didn't know it.

Nine years later, in 1741, Bering sailed as straight to the east as winds would allow and saw Mount Saint Elias, on the modern border between Alaska and Canada. A naturalist on the voyage, Georg Steller, recognized a jay as a New World species. The bird sighting confirmed that the expedition had reached North America.

By the reign of Alexander I the government-chartered Russian-American Company had established a precarious toe-hold in the area now called Alaska. The company shipped furs of animals harvested by indigenous Aleut and Tlingit hunters. It operated a handful of wood forts staffed by a few hundred armed Russians, mostly convicts and Cossacks. (The Yup'ik Eskimo word for any person of European descent is still "Kass'aq.")

The future Alexander II was born in 1818, a nephew of Alexander I. It was not obvious that he would be in line for the throne. But the two daughters of Alexander I died early. When Alexander himself died in 1825 the next in succession was his brother, Konstantin, Governor General of Poland. But Konstantin Pavlovich declined the dangerous honor. So the throne passed to Alexander's next-oldest brother, Nicholas, the father of Alexander II.

The last years of Alexander I had seen two important treaties signed regarding Russian America. The first, in 1824, concerned trading rights with the Americans. Yankee traders had been increasingly active in the Pacific Northwest, often handling the shipment of Russian furs to China, where Russia itself was not allowed to do business.

It was a complicated arrangement. The Americans had lost their only West Coast settlement, Astoria on the Columbia River, to the British in the War of 1812. The Russians had established Fort Ross, just north of San Francisco, in part to grow food for their Alaska outposts. Spain, then Mexico, claimed the entire Pacific coast, but had few ships to enforce their claims.

The second treaty, with England in 1825, set the border between Russian and British territory in Northwest America. Russia retained the 300-mile archipelago north of the Queen Charlotte Islands and a narrow band of mainland, but British ships could navigate the waters to supply their own outposts. Rival fur companies of both nations quietly agreed to avoid hostilities with one another.

Almost as an afterthought, a north-south line was drawn beginning at Mount Saint Elias and continuing to the Arctic Ocean, cutting through country that neither British nor Russians had ever seen. That long, straight line remains the border between Alaska and Canada. It is the longest national frontier that has never been crossed by an army intent on attacking its neighbor.

Nicholas I (1796-1855) would not know such peace elsewhere in his realm.

He had been given a solid grounding in military tactics and pomp. But unlike his two older brothers, he had not received much instruction in administration, diplomacy and liberal arts. He was known as a good-natured, by-the-book guy with little in the way of a strong personality. It seemed that Nicholas would become the puppet of whichever faction could assert itself most forcefully and quickly.

The first faction to try was a group of officers in the Palace Guard, the corps that had backed every successful palace coup since putting Elizabeth in power in 1741. On a cold December day, before Nicholas could be crowned, they assembled in battle gear near the Winter Palace. Their leaders demanded his abdication and the creation of a constitutional republic. A mob gathered. Attempts to disperse them by officials and churchmen failed; the would-be negotiators fled in fear for their lives.

Nicholas and his family, including little Alexander, were trapped in the palace. For several hours it seemed that the Romanov dynasty would end at nightfall. But at the last moment a unit loyal to the new Tsar arrived. Nicholas ordered cannons turned on the mutineers and the rebellion was quashed.

Shaken by how close he had come to being deposed and likely executed, Nicholas shed the complacency he had previously displayed and became one of the most detail-attentive and suspicious rulers of any country ever. The Decembrist revolutionaries were killed or sent to hard labor. Freedom of movement was severely restricted, freedom of press abolished. "Orthodoxy, Autocracy, Nationality" became an official doctrine, with heavy emphasis on the middle word.

Nicholas' Russia was a nation of stifling intellectual silence. No one could speak his mind. The Third Department, the secret police, censored writing inside the country, prohibited the importation of books from outside and put spies everywhere. Initiative dared not show itself except in the nefarious form of creative — and sometimes blatant — corruption. In eerie ways it resembled the Soviet Union under Stalin in the next century.

Nicholas was as strict with himself as he was with his subordinates. He slept on a rude iron army cot. He relaxed in a field coat rather than a robe or a dressing gown.

He didn't relax much. He knew his brother had been part of the plot that killed his father in his own bedroom. He knew it was fatal for a Tsar to be caught sleeping.

Three: The Tsarevich Goes to School

Alexander Nikolayevich, "Sasha" to the family, was eight years old when he became Tsarevich, the heir to the throne.

Perhaps reflecting on his own limited schooling, Nicholas made sure that his son would get a well-rounded education. Nicholas may have been strict, but he was not stupid. He wanted his successor to be prepared for the duties that awaited a future Tsar.

Sasha's main tutor was a poet, Vassily Andreyevich Zhukovsky. Zhukovsky was an old school romantic whose patriotic verses became popular during Napoleon's invasion of Russia in 1812. He came into the royal household as a translator of German poetry. Russian rulers typically sought German brides and the women brought their love of German authors with them.

Zhukovsky called his lessons "journeys." He was a devoted Christian who stressed the importance of compassion to his royal student. Tsar Nicholas, who had to approve everything, often scolded him for lesson plans he found too soft.

Other teachers of the top order joined Zhukovsky in teaching Sasha a catalog of subjects that reads like a college curriculum: history, physics, geology, philosophy, jurisprudence, math and, of course, military science.

The Tsarevich also had to absorb French, German, English and Polish. In addition there were the aesthetic and athletic skills of art, music, dancing, fencing, swimming, gymnastics and even the humble but practical skill of woodworking.

Each morning Sasha woke at 6 a.m., dressed in a military uniform and arrived in class with two appointed companions, sons of courtiers, at 7 a.m. Studies went uninterrupted for five hours. Then came a two-hour walk around St. Petersburg in which he was to observe buildings and people, "The book of Russia," as Zhukovsky called it. The group regularly read poetry aloud during their strolls.

Lunch followed, then the lessons resumed for two more hours until 5 p.m. After an hour of rest the young men went on to physical training and sports before dinner at 10 p.m. The day ended with prayers.

War training was a must for the son of Nicholas. Young Sasha proved to be an excellent horseman and, at age 13, was made a captain of the Cadet Corps. He reveled in parades and elaborate military reviews. While he trembled at any sign of disapproval from his father, the most demeaning punishment Nicholas held over his head was suspending his right to wear a uniform for a month.

The busy Emperor had little time for his son, however. Sasha spent more time with his sensitive but shallow mother, Alexandra. She was born Charlotte, daughter of the King of Prussia, and changed her name when she converted to Orthodoxy in order to marry into the Romanovs. The two countries had a long history of hostilities and alliances.

Alexandra seemed content with her glittering life of palaces and balls. Nicholas was well pleased with a wife who didn't think too much. For intimacy, however, he turned to his mistress, who lived in the Winter Palace with the royal family. When Sasha found out he was horrified and perplexed.

Things cleared up for him when he became a teenager.

He fell in love for the first time at age 14. His inamorata was a lady-in-waiting. They flung themselves at each other, being too young to know how to hide it. Even Otto von Bismarck, Prussia's ambassador to St. Petersburg at the time, could see the Tsarevich's passion written on his face. The royal parents saw the same signs and the young lady was sent off to a forced marriage.

At the age of 18 Sasha completed his classroom studies and was sent on a tour of the country. "Familiarize yourself with the state you will rule sooner or later," wrote Nicholas. "Avoid making remarks. You are traveling not to judge, but to learn."

For the next seven months, everywhere he went, the heir was welcomed by throngs that numbered in the thousands. Crowds pressed on him in the Urals. He sat at the tables of peasants in their huts on the steppes. He became the first future Tsar to travel to Siberia. In all, he visited 30 provinces on a route that did not extend even halfway across the gigantic country.

Arriving at a small Siberian backwater in 1837 he saw a cluster of miserable wretches in the back of a church. The priest bowed toward the group when he came to the part of the liturgy that included petitions for prisoners. The men were Decembrists, sent into exile after their failed rebellion against Alexander's father, Tsar Nicholas, in 1825. The Tsarevich was touched by their plight and wrote to his father on their behalf.

Nicholas transferred them from Siberia to fight in the Caucasus, where a bitter war was raging against Muslim mountaineers. At the moment, the mountaineers had the upper hand. This was the Tsar's idea of mercy.

But his son was delighted to know that he had asked a favor of his father that had been granted, however curtly.

Four: Love and Marriage

Alexander's love interest, a young Queen Victoria of England

In December of 1837, shortly after Alexander returned to St. Petersburg, the Winter Palace and port facilities caught fire at the same time. Alexander went galloping through the streets to take command of the firefighters at the port. The blaze was extinguished by morning with relatively limited damage.

The Winter Palace, however, went up in flames that one eyewitness compared to a volcano. Nicholas ordered it to be rebuilt within a year. Serfs labored in temperatures of 20 below zero. Hundreds died. But the work was completed on schedule. The Tsar's word was absolute, even when he demanded the unreasonable.

The palace reopened with familiar rounds of protocol and ceremonies. But Alexander had grown during his seven months outside his father's immediate control. It was now time for another trip, this one to Europe, and with a specific purpose — to find a bride.

He looked over his cousins in Prussia. He met the beauties of Austria at the home of Prince Klemens von Metternich, the architect of the peace that Europe enjoyed for three decades following the defeat of Napoleon. He traveled in Italy. In the little German duchy of Hesse-Darmstadt he found a deliciously pretty 14-year-old princess, Maximiliana-Wilhelmina-Augusta-Sophie. He wrote his father excitedly and then continued his journey.

The next stop was England, intended more as a state visit than a wife-hunting expedition. But the unexpected happened when he set eyes on Queen Victoria.

Victoria, who had begun her long reign at the same time that Alexander was touring Russia, was 20 years old and still unmarried. The elegant, cultured, witty young Queen and the handsome, manly Tsarevich, who could never conceal his affections, were instantly attracted to each other.

"I really am quite in love with the Grand Duke," Victoria wrote in her diary, using his formal title. She praised his "fine figure" and "sweet smile." They met behind a curtain at her box at the opera. They danced into the early hours of the morning. "I never enjoyed myself more," she wrote. The ball ended at 2 a.m. but she couldn't fall asleep until dawn.

Palace chatter ran that, if he were to propose, the Queen would readily accept. Romantically, it would seem like a match made for a sparkling operetta.

Nicholas saw it as the prologue to an epic Greek tragedy.

The calf-eyed lovers couldn't see the insurmountable difficulty of separating national interests from family ties when monarchs marry each other. Victoria was hardly likely to move to St. Petersburg and accept the subordinate role of Tsarina. Nor was it in Russia's interest for the future Tsar to renounce his throne in order to live in London as a mere Prince Consort.

Nicholas sent word approving the marriage with the girl from Hesse-Darmstadt. Alexander met with Victoria a final time.

"He looked pale and his voice faltered," she wrote. "He then pressed and kissed my hand, and I kissed his cheek." Alexander then kissed her cheek "in a very warm affectionate manner, and we again warmly shook hands. I felt so sad."

Alexander, who loved his dogs and often included them in his official portraits, gave her his favorite, Kazbek. She kept it with her for the rest of its life, even after she married her cousin Albert two years later.

The Tsarevich returned to St. Petersburg with his German princess. The court whispered about whether her birth and title were legitimate, sniped at her looks and her poor French. But Nicholas liked her. She was polite, punctual, respectful and, most importantly, obedient.

At a glance from the Tsar, the rumors stopped.

She was received into the Orthodox Church, changed her name to Maria Alexandrovna and bore six sons and two daughters. Oldest son Nicholas Alexandrovich, the heir apparent, was particularly bright and spirited. He was still a tyke when he brashly proclaimed that he would declare war on Europe.

His namesake grandfather liked him, too.

Five: Revolts and Revenge

No one crossed Tsar Nicholas. Nonetheless, the palace contained two camps that should be explained in the context of the period. The liberals were those who thought that open exchanges of ideas, decentralization of government, laissez-faire business rules and some form of popular input into the government would have a beneficial effect. Conservatives felt that any attempt to institute any unwise changes would, in Russia, lead to chaos and the end of the state.

Sasha's aunt, Elena Pavlovna, the German-born wife of the Tsar's younger brother Mikhail, was a liberal and one of the few people Nicholas allowed to disagree with him. A brilliant intellectual, she held salons that drew the cream of Russian scholars. She distributed her lavish patronage to hospitals and the arts.

The other liberal in the family was Sasha's younger brother, Konstantin Nikolayevich. Educated with the same degree of attention that his brother had received, Konstantin was known for his conceit and sharp tongue. Even in the face of his father's wrath, he could be counted on to stick to his own ideas, some of which were downright radical. Groomed to take over command of the navy, he would play an important role in the future of Russia's colony across the Bering Sea.

Russian America, with its tiny population of settlers and who-knew-how-many indigenous residents, was not a priority for Nicholas. It was the one part of his empire about which he seemed to hold no strong opinion. Debate over whether the colony was worth the effort was tolerated as a business matter, not a squarely political issue such as would have required his attention.

Nicholas raised no objection when the Russian-American Company's southernmost post, Fort Ross, was sold to a Swiss immigrant, John Sutter, in 1841. He may have felt a twinge of regret a few years later when gold was found at Sutter's Mill. But the onslaught of unruly, armed Americans into California in numbers that Russia could never have matched suggested that the Russian-American Company had cleared out just in time to avoid being appropriated, the way the rest of Alta California — consisting of the territory from today's state of California to the Rocky Mountains — was taken from Mexico.

The fact that the Americans began to put pressure on British interests in Oregon — and, soon enough, western Canada — was, from Nicholas' point of view, a good thing.

His more urgent priority was keeping millions of subjects under control on his own continent. Though no one dared to openly suggest that things were less than sunny, he was aware that discontent rumbled throughout the empire. He had the Third Department prepare a report on the status of the country. In it, the head of the secret police compared the serfs to "a cellar of gunpowder under the state."

Dissatisfaction with rulers was not restricted to Russia. All over Europe the lower and middle classes were chafing at exploitation. The wealthy acted unconcerned or unaware of their condition. But among the oppressed were people who could read and write. Papers were circulating. Talk of democracy, law and justice grew louder every day.

In 1848 the toxic talk metastasized into violent action. Beginning in February, French reformers and workers took to the streets. Within weeks revolts had spread from Italy to Germany and even to South America. The rulers were caught by surprise. King Louis Philippe of France fled to England, the last monarch in the line that had ruled the country for nearly 900 years.

Other kings trembled in their palaces. Among them was Franz Josef, Emperor of Austria, whose Hungarian province was in the throes of a widespread popular uprising and threatened to split off on its own.

Fortunately for the royalists, the revolts were not well-coordinated. As the revolutionaries quarreled among themselves the forces of tradition and wealth regrouped and pushed back. The counterattack in France came in June. Ten thousand people were killed or injured. Four thousand were deported to Algeria. Uprisings were crushed in nation after nation.

But Hungary remained stubbornly independent. In June of 1849 Franz Josef begged Nicholas to help him. The Tsar had the largest standing army on the continent. He poured troops into Hungary, where the overwhelmed defenders surrendered on August 13. The Austrian Empire was saved.

Nicholas used the victory to set an example for any of his subjects who might think of causing trouble. A hundred or so Hungarian men were shot. Their women supporters were flogged in public. Theaters were closed. Public gatherings were outlawed. No one was allowed to wear national costumes.

Although the revolutionary fervor cooled, the uprisings nonetheless had a democratizing effect in most of Europe. Grievances had been heard and some in the ruling class insisted changes must be made. Absolute monarchy ended in Denmark. Parliamentary elections came to the Netherlands. Serfdom was abolished in the parts of Eastern Europe where it had continued. Restrictions on press and speech were eased.

Some outside of Hungary used their new freedoms to protest that Nicholas had gone too far. He was criticized by foreign politicians and writers in terms that would not be tolerated in his own country.

The Tsar fully expected he would be seen as a savior. Instead, much to his consternation, he found himself branded as a tyrannical bully.

Attacks in the foreign press could not cause trouble among his subjects. No one in Russia had the bad sense to side with the revolutionaries. The nation felt as stable as ever, at least on the surface.

Still, Nicholas burned with indignation at the ingratitude of his fellow monarchs. He resolved to wait for an opportunity to claw back their respect.

In 1853 he thought he saw that opportunity. It would lead to the greatest mistake of his life.

Six: Pride Before the Fall

For centuries Russia's Tsars looked southward to Turkey with yearning and fear. They yearned for access to the Mediterranean Sea, to sail their merchant ships and navy through the straits of the Bosporus without the possibility of being choked off at Constantinople. But they feared the might of the Ottoman domain that stretched from Africa to Persia, an empire that included the Balkans and provinces of Eastern Europe at the mouth of the Danube.

More than mere territory and trade was at stake. Constantinople held an almost mythic position in Russian lore. The Crown of Monomakh worn by the ancient Tsars was said to have been a gift from a Byzantine Emperor. The Tsars considered themselves the successors of the Roman Caesars. The head of the Russian Orthodox Church, the Metropolitan of Moscow, was considered the heir of the Patriarch of Constantinople.

Muslims had long ruled the city built by Roman Emperor Constantine and the historical connection with Russia was, frankly, tenuous. Nonetheless, Russians saw it as a sacred part of their patrimony. It was the rightful imperial capital, lost through the perfidy and indifference of Western Europeans. The Tsars dreamed of a time when they would return Constantinople to Christendom and an Orthodox Emperor would again rule from the banks of the Bosporus.

But by the 19th century, most of Europe saw the Ottoman Empire as a trading partner rather than as a military threat. As long as the Turks remained neutral and treated all sides fairly, everyone prospered.

Fair trade was especially important to Russia, whose main export product was grain. Most of that grain went to world markets down the Don River to Azov, guarded by the Crimean Peninsula. From there it was shipped to world markets through the straits at Constantinople. Russia had sent thousands of soldiers to their deaths in order to acquire that strategically critical peninsula — and it wanted more.

In addition to the geopolitical stakes was the fact that a sizable minority of Ottoman subjects in the Middle East and Egypt were Orthodox Christians. In Eastern Europe they were a majority. By custom and treaty, the Tsar was their protector. With the permission of their Muslim rulers, Orthodox clergy had custody of the sacred Christian sites in the Holy Land.

But there were also a small number of Catholics living under Turkish rule, a vestige from the Crusades. When France became a republic after the events of 1848, Louis Napoleon, nephew of the Emperor Napoleon Bonaparte, was elected President. He started plotting to become France's next Emperor. Needing the support of his religious constituents, he prevailed on the Turks to let Catholics take control of the holy sites in 1851.

The Sultan, who perhaps never imagined that two groups of Christians would come to blows, acquiesced. Fighting broke out between Orthodox and Catholic monks at the Church of the Nativity in Bethlehem. Several people were killed.

The Tsar blamed the Turks. He demanded that the sites be returned to Orthodox clergy. When the Sultan refused, Nicholas acted on his authority as protector of the Christians under Turkish rule and, in the summer of 1853, sent troops into Ottoman territory at the mouth of the Danube River.

The Turks responded by declaring war and massed their military to repel the invaders. The ground battle was inconclusive, but in November Russian warships destroyed much of the Turkish fleet in the Battle of Sinope, on the north coast of Turkey. It was the last major naval battle fought exclusively between sailing ships. Nicholas did not believe in the new-fangled steam engines.

The loss of ships made it impossible for Turkey to supply its troops on the other side of the Black Sea. This gave Russia a powerful advantage. England and France, which had urged Turkey to confront Russia, now felt obliged to step in and rescue their Ottoman ally. They declared war early in 1854, demanding that Nicholas retreat from the Danube even as they built up their forces.

Austria also felt nervous about having a large Russian army so close. Franz Joseph did not declare war, but neither did he promise to remain neutral. In fact the Austrian government let it be known that its sympathies lay with Turkey.

Nicholas seethed at the betrayal by Austria, the nation he had saved in 1848. Nonetheless, he withdrew his troops while the British and French were still assembling an expeditionary army.

A rational observer might conclude that hostilities should have ended right then and there. But it was too late. Newspapers in Britain and France had whipped up war fever among their populations. Both nations saw some advantage in grinding down the Russian colossus. An allied armada of warships and men sailed into the Black Sea and prepared to storm the naval base at Sevastopol.

After all the hoopla, they couldn't be ordered home just because the reason for the war no longer existed.

Seven: Catastrophe in Crimea

Ruins of Sevastopol, from the Library of Congresss.

In September of 1854, 60,000 allied troops landed on the Crimean Peninsula. It was a chaotic scene with three different armies under three different commands, none of which seemed to know what the other was doing.

"The French, though they had tents, had no cavalry; the Turks had neither cavalry nor food; the British had cavalry, but they had neither tents nor transport, nor ambulances nor litters." So wrote William Howard Russell, a writer covering the war for **The Times** of London.

Russell's on-the-spot reporting marked the beginning of modern journalism. Using the telegraph, he shot dispatches back to his editors in England within hours and updated the army's progress — or lack of it — daily.

There was much to report, and much of it was embarrassing.

"While the French and British troops consider their most harassing work to be the duty in the trenches, the Turks ... do not take any share in actual siege operations and amuse themselves with the mere pastime of foraging or actually sitting in indolence for hours," he wrote.

English law let Russell write what he saw and what he wrote gave the government fits. Queen Victoria thought he should face criminal charges. But the public gobbled up the scandals and shouted for the heads of those responsible.

On the other side of the battle lines, Nicholas chortled, "We have no need for spies. We have ***The Times!***"

In America today the Crimean War is remembered for two things. One is Alfred Tennyson's poem "The Charge of the Light Brigade," a ringing indictment of senseless bloodshed and command incompetence. The other is the work of Florence Nightingale, "the lady with the lamp," whose efforts to assist injured allied soldiers near the front gave birth to the Red Cross.

In fact it was a war of many firsts. The first to use electronic communications. The first to be captured on camera. The first to use torpedoes, rail transportation and hospital trains.

The Russians had their own Florence Nightingales. Grand Duchess Elena Pavlovna, ever involved with charities and missions of mercy, organized companies of women nurses for the defenders of Sevastopol. In addition, the leading Russian surgeon, Nikolay Pirogov, made advances in the use of plaster casts, improved amputation techniques, a refined triage system and — to the unspeakable gratitude of many a wounded Russian — brought anesthesia to a battlefield for the first time in history.

The Russians on the peninsula were seriously outnumbered and they were fighting with inferior technology. The British had tents made 40 years earlier, but their rifles were the latest in weaponry. The flintlocks in the hands of Nicholas' soldiers were the same as their predecessors had held when they faced Napoleon Bonaparte's Grande Armée. The aging Russian cannons could not fire as fast, as far or as accurately as those of their enemies.

The allied navies were stymied in their attempt to seize the mouth of the Don River, the strategic waterway east of Crimea, flowing into the Sea of Azov from the north. Local boatmen relocated buoys and the invaders' ships ran around. Nonetheless, the allies controlled the water approaches to the Crimea and made resupply of Sevastopol difficult.

Against all odds, the Russians held back the allies until winter closed in. Though the Crimean winter was nothing like the blizzards that destroyed Napoleon on his retreat from Moscow, the allies were not prepared for it. Sickness stalked the camps and killed many times more soldiers than would die in combat. France lost 10,000 killed on the field, another 20,000 from wounds and 75,000 to illness.

Russell's reports of official stupidity brought down the British government. Facing an investigation by Parliament, Prime Minister George Hamilton-Gordon, the Earl of Aberdeen, resigned in 1855. The weary besiegers encamped before Sevastopol lost their spirit.

"A very pretty little rebellion sprang up among the (Indian) drivers of the Land Transport Corps of the Fourth Division," Russell reported. "They would not stir in spite of eloquent exhortations in the best Hindostanee addressed to them by Captain Dick, who, standing knee deep in snow and mud harangued them as they lay inside their tents. They sahibbed away and shrugged their shoulders and plaintively expressed a decided desire to be flogged accompanied by suggestions also that they should be at once executed, but they one and all declared that work they would not on such a raw and gusty day."

And yet the allied powers could not withdraw. A railroad was under construction to bring in more big guns and endless ammunition. Eventually Sevastopol would be under round-the-clock bombardment and subject to repeated attempts to storm the walls by endless ranks of French and British soldiers whose officers had finally learned how to fight a war.

The Tsar dispatched Alexander to the city to report on conditions. The Tsarevich returned with grim news to deliver to a man whom no one, not even his own son, had ever dared to contradict.

Alexander trembled, expecting to be the victim of his father's fury. But he had imbibed from Zhukovsky the code of Christian knighthood. Honor compelled him to present the facts and speak frankly, no matter the cost. He could not lie about what he had seen.

Sevastopol would fall, he said. It would fall and there was nothing the Tsar could do about it. Thousands of Russians had perished in a lost cause.

Hearing this news, Nicholas' steel left him. He wept as he realized the mistake he'd made by surrounding himself with people who were afraid to tell him the truth. In the days that followed he seemed to give up on life. He became ill and took to his iron army cot, where he died, apparently at peace, in February of 1855.

Alexander now had to take the seat below the sword of Damocles. The throne would come with many problems that had festered during his father's reign. But the biggest problem by far was the war.

It had to be stopped at all costs, regardless of what that might mean to Russian pride.

Eight: A World War

O ne important legal detail had to be cleared up before Alexander could be crowned. His uncle Konstantin was still alive and could, in theory, reclaim the right of succession he had renounced 30 years before. In fact the old man was, if anything, even more eager to avoid the responsibilities than he had been when he insisted that his younger brother Nicholas take the crown.

By the standards of the imperial bureaucracy, the transition went smoothly and quickly. But not quickly enough to save Sevastopol. Within weeks after Nicholas' death, the allies had their railway completed and giant cannons were rolling into position. They would subject Sevastopol to a bombing the likes of which would not be seen again until World War I.

The Russians evacuated at the end of the summer. The victorious allies marched into a trophy of rubble.

The Crimean War has been called "the first of the World Wars" because of the number of nations involved and because of the several fronts where fighting took place. The Black Sea was only one theater of action. The allies also attacked through the Arctic Ocean, sailing into the White Sea and firing cannonballs at ports — and a monastery. The strategic value was minimal, but by showing they could strike such a remote target well inside the Russian border, the British navy delivered a powerful psychological slap.

More frightening for St. Petersburg was the assault on maritime facilities in the Baltic Sea. As Sevastopol was falling in the south, an allied fleet knocked out the fortress of Bomarsund in the north. The warships were within striking distance of Russia's capital, which was woefully unprepared to defend itself.

The invaders conducted several small raids, then turned 1,000 guns on the dockyards near Helsinki, for Finland was a Russian vassal state at the time. Over two days the attackers sent some 20,000 rounds into shore defenses.

The plucky Finns refused to surrender. A single Russian ship with only 120 cannons managed to block the narrow entrance to the harbor. The allies withdrew and assembled a new fleet of 350 gunboats, nearly three times as many keels as sailed in the Spanish Armada of 1588 and possessing far more firepower.

The war was over before they could return to action. The loyalty of the Finns in Russia's hour of need would not be forgotten.

The other place where Russia could claim a victory was on the Pacific front. The dream of a good Asian port had been pursued since the days of Peter the Great. The Siberian coast held few prospects. The best harbor, Petropavlovsk-Kamchatsky, was located on the Kamchatka Peninsula and involved a long, out-of-the way, overland trip. The situation made shipping between Russian America and the mother country difficult, risky and tenuous.

A more practical route to the Pacific was the 3,000 mile long Amur River between Siberia and China. But no one knew much about it. A 1689 treaty prohibited any ships on the waterway.

Upon signing the treaty, China had moved all of its subjects out of the area lest they become contaminated with non-Chinese ideas. They placed a fort at one end to remind Russians that they were forbidden to set foot there. Nothing happened in the Amur Valley for more than 100 years. Meanwhile, in the north, Russia expanded eastward and claimed a piece of America.

In 1847 Nicholas appointed Nikolay Muravyov to be Governor of Irkutsk and Eastern Siberia. The sparsely-settled country amounted to roughly one third of Russia's land mass. Muravyov saw in it the nation's future. His success would have a decisive impact on the fate of Russian America.

Muravyov justified the Tsar's trust in him. He stopped the embezzlement of government money that had been rampant in the distant and often lawless region. He organized new settlements and explorations of the area, improved schools and harnessed the power of local religions — whether Christianity, Buddhism or shamanism — to the interests of the state.

Insofar as he could tell, the Amur looked suitable for vessels. But no one could say where it reached the ocean or whether the mouth was navigable. The Russian-American Company was instructed to conduct a secret mission.

Disguising their ship and themselves as Americans, a crew from New Archangel found the estuary of the Amur west of Sakhalin Island and determined its suitability for boat traffic. The local people told them no one could recall ever having seen any Chinese in the area.

The report was kept secret while Muravyov prepared a grand expedition over the objections of ministers who feared the wrath of China. The status quo had worked fine, they said. Who knew how many soldiers Beijing might have in the area?

Muravyov couldn't answer that question, but he was determined to claim the Amur for Russia. Nicholas gave his approval as long as the Governor could make his move without triggering a second war.

With astonishing speed, Muravyov built a shipyard at inland Irkutsk. As the ice left the river in May of 1854 he sent a flotilla of 77 barges led by a steamship to the mouth of the river where the Russian navy, with a few settlers brought over from New Archangel, had established the town of Nikolayevsk-on-Amur.

Muravyov planned to stay. The barges carried soldiers and cannons, partly in anticipation of trouble from the Chinese. But there were no Chinese troops along the river; Beijing had long before decided they weren't necessary.

On his way back, he stopped by the Chinese fortress at Aigun and told the startled garrison to expect Russian boats on the Amur. He sent a message to Beijing saying a new treaty was needed. Russia was now at war with Britain and would not tolerate any infringement of its right to defend itself.

The Chinese, who had recently been given a black eye by the British in the Opium War, were inclined to consent. The Treaty of Aigun wouldn't actually be signed until after the Crimean War was over but a second treaty, signed in Beijing in 1860, would expand on it, making the Amur the official boundary of the two countries. Russia would have free access to the Pacific and possession of the provinces that now make up the country's southeast corner.

But fighting lay ahead. Even as Muravyov pioneered the route down the Amur, a joint French and British fleet set course to seize Petropavlovsk. The cannons and soldiers brought down the river in barges were moved to the Kamchatka and braced for a battle they couldn't hope to win.

They didn't have long to wait.

Nine: A Humiliating Peace

In August six allied warships commanded by British Rear-Admiral David Price came in sight of Petropavlovsk. Price had 2,600 troops with him. The Russians numbered about 900, counting sailors, hunters and workmen pressed into service. The invaders had 218 top-of-the-line cannons. The defenders had 67, most of them old.

Price was a poor commander. Due to his incompetence the fleet was behind schedule. That gave Muravyov time to prepare a resistance and move most of his ships to safety.

Just before the attack, the British leader went below deck and experienced an unfortunate incident with a handgun. He died by accident or suicide; the evidence is inconclusive. French Rear-Admiral Auguste Febvrier-Despointes took command.

An allied force of nearly 1,000 regular troops, backed up by sailors, landed west of the town. They were pushed back into the sea by 360 Russians. A second landing party of nearly 700 was ambushed as it came ashore. With winter approaching, Febvrier-Despointes called off the attack and sailed west to British Columbia.

Thirty-one Russians died in the siege. British and French dead were estimated at 500. A French reporter called it "a shameful rout." The Siege of Petropavlovsk is not mentioned in most British accounts of the Crimean War.

En route to Vancouver Island, the allied fleet sailed within a few hundred miles of Russian America. Had Febvrier-Despointes made the detour, New Archangel would easily have fallen. The English would have claimed it as a spoil of war. It's unlikely that they would have been inclined to sell the obvious extension of Canada at any cost. Alaska would today be part of the British Commonwealth.

As it was, the truce between the Hudson's Bay and Russian-American companies held, even as their countrymen around the globe shot, bombed and bayoneted each other.

The next year the allies returned to Siberia and conducted a series of small raids. Muravyov had evacuated Petropavlovsk while the snow was still on the ground. The cannons were moved to defend Nikolayevsk.

The allies knew nothing about the new settlements on the Amur. Febvrier-Despointes departed the North Pacific wondering why the Russian boats he was sure he'd spied seemed to vanish as if by magic.

While the combatants played peek-a-boo in the Pacific, the serious business of negotiating a peace was underway on the other side of the world. The French and English governments, pilloried by their own press over the incompetence of their commanders, were as anxious to end things as the battered Russians.

But it was not pleasant business for the new Tsar's diplomats. The terms imposed by the allies were humiliating. The Treaty of Paris, signed in March of 1856, restored to Turkey much of the land Russia had taken. Russia also had to give up territory at the mouth of the Danube. Neither Turkey nor Russia could establish forts around the Black Sea. Both nations were prohibited from stationing warships there. Alexander had to pledge to respect the borders of the Ottoman Empire.

As he swallowed the indignity, Alexander reassured himself that it would not last forever. He knew alliances form, shatter and reform over time. When he met prisoners of war in Sevastopol the French had pleaded with him to separate them from those beastly British prisoners. He had only to wait until the English, French and Prussians were at each others' throats to re-evaluate his options.

He could take comfort in the fact that he had gained more territory in the Far East than he had lost on the Black Sea. The shell-pocked Crimea and Sevastopol were handed back to him by the treaty. And, while the Danube principalities of Wallachia and Moldavia, with their large Christian populations, remained with Turkey, they had essentially become independent. The Slavs of the Ottoman Empire looked to Russia's Tsar as their promised savior even more hopefully than they had before the war.

Finally, although the Western powers that had dictated the terms didn't see it, the Treaty of Paris gift-wrapped a grand prize for the Russians. It made no mention of the Caucasus.

The conquest of the region had stalled during the Crimean conflict. Now Alexander was free to resume the unfinished business.

He did it brutally.

Ten: The Circassian Extermination

The Caucasus Mountain Range rises like a wall running from the Black Sea to the Caspian Sea. It contains a jumble of disputed semi-states like Chechnya, Ossetia and Dagestan, places that continue to be trouble spots in our own time.

The region had long served as a buffer between Turkey, which considered itself the protector of the area's Muslim tribes, and Russia, which saw the region as an opportunity for expansion and a strategic asset in its ongoing wars with the Turks.

Around the same time as the American Revolution, Catherine the Great ordered her generals to conquer the region. She built a chain of fortresses and a broad highway through the middle of the range by which her army could be supplied and reinforced.

Catherine's campaigns had limited success. Each valley had its own tribe that thought of itself as an independent nation. Every man had a rifle. Each was ready to fight to the death. The Russian army was vexed by snow and forests and steep terrain. Fighting subsided in the early years of the 19th century when the threat of Napoleon forced Russia to turn its attention toward Europe. The Caucasus was left simmering in an uneasy stalemate.

In 1828 the long series of wars with the Ottoman Empire resumed. Nicholas used the occasion to ratchet up operations in the Caucasus. The Treaty of Adrianople put a temporary halt to hostilities with Turkey the following year and left the Tsar free to throw his forces against the mountaineers.

Using guerrilla tactics, local Muslims held their own. Resistance was particularly intense in the western part of the mountains, Circassia.

A leader, Imam Shamil, arose and united the diverse tribes. A savvy strategist, he was fearless in battle. He personally led sorties against the Russians and had numerous wounds to show for it. He expected no mercy and showed none.

Like the British in India, the Russians found it easy to seize a state ruled by a single despot. To acquire a khanate one had only to capture or compromise the Khan. But the mountainous nations did not answer to any monarch. Nicholas could not negotiate with a dependable authority. He faced a potential battlefield behind every rock and inside every house.

Britain had learned the peril of pursuing war in the region the hard way. In 1842 a force of 16,500 soldiers and camp followers was whittled to a single survivor as it attempted to retreat from Afghanistan. Similarly, in Circassia, Russian troops shuddered to find the mutilated bodies of massacred comrades.

The Caucasus got a short reprieve when the Revolutions of 1848 diverted the Tsar's attention. Shamil was at the height of his power.

Shortly after suppressing the Hungarian revolt, Nicholas sent his son into combat. Alexander is known to have taken part in at least one battle that involved hand-to-hand combat. The Russians took heavy casualties in the melee. Every Muslim fighter was killed.

The Tsarevich had now seen blood. He would see much more in the decades that followed his father's death.

Alexander was crowned amid elaborate festivities in Moscow in August of 1856. He wasted no time in taking out Russia's frustration over the Crimean War on the Circassians.

The warriors of the Caucasus had fought on the side of Turkey. They assumed Turkey's allies would protect them after Russia's defeat. They were wrong. The British expressed sympathy. They did not like to see the Tsar edging toward India. But the once-boiling fever for war had chilled into broad anti-war sentiment.

Learning from the mistakes of Crimea, Alexander upgraded the weapons available to his men. Tactics were re-evaluated. Instead of looking for a fight against organized ranks or waiting in their forts, the Russians began a scorched-earth policy. Any place where a resistance fighter might hide was considered a fair target. Villages were razed. Fields, crops and livestock were systematically destroyed. Entire families and populations were executed, including women and children.

Shamil responded in kind, attacking Russian villages or villages that had accepted Russian rule. But the mountaineers could not hold back the tens of thousands of invaders who ravaged the country and claimed it one smoldering acre at a time. The Circassians retreated into the most remote part of the mountains. The Russians followed, slaughtering every non-Russian along the way.

By August of 1859 Shamil's army was reduced to an exhausted 400 men trapped in the hamlet of Gunib. The Russian commander drew up his ranks and prepared to lose at least as many soldiers as there were defenders. But first he made a final offer for the guerrilla leader to surrender.

Shamil was ready to die, but none of his men were. Even his sons, listening to the cries of the women begging for their lives, told him they had had enough. In the end Shamil walked out and prepared to be killed.

Instead he and his wives and children were sent to St. Petersburg, a journey of 1,500 miles. As he passed through the vast farmlands and great cities, Shamil began to realize the enormity of the power he had resisted for so many years.

He still expected to be executed when his captors presented him to Alexander. But the Tsar greeted him in the spirit of chivalry. He embraced the old warrior, gave him money and a black bear coat and handed out gifts to his family.

Shamil spent his final years living openly in Kiev, something of a celebrity in his ostentatious turban as he rode around in a fine carriage. He died on pilgrimage to Mecca in 1871.

The war in the Caucasus did not end immediately. Resistance continued. The final solution came in the form of mass deportations that began in 1857 and continued into the 1860s.

Those who did not surrender were killed. Those who didn't fight were driven out in a policy to "cleanse the land of hostile elements." Entire Circassian populations were sent to the plains to become farmers or sent into Ottoman territory. In the process thousands of civilians were massacred. By 1864 the Caucasus was declared pacified — and virtually empty of people.

The numbers are hard to nail down. Various sources calculate that 100,000 Russians perished in the Circassian War. Eight hundred thousand Circassians died. Another 200,000 were resettled in Russia. Most of the survivors, however, chose to go to other Muslim territory. According to Circassian historian Amjad Jaimoukha, anywhere between 500,000 and 2,000,000 Caucasus Muslims left for the Ottoman Empire. Twenty percent perished in the exodus. Today an estimated 600 villages in modern Turkey are considered to be populated by ethnic Circassians.

The Circassian genocide, for such it must be called, was a stark departure from the usual Russian policy. In Central Asia, Siberia and elsewhere indigenous populations were repressed, but also assimilated.

Circassia, however, was pacified through ruthless ethnic cleansing.

In fact such massacres and deportations were acceptable acts of war in the 19th century, not substantially different from the actions taken by the Europeans against Africans or the United States against American Indians. Nonetheless, if the extermination of Circassia were the only achievement of Alexander's reign, he would probably be remembered as a monster on the scale of Ivan the Terrible or Stalin.

Instead, posterity praises him as one of Russia's greatest humanitarians.

Alexander II as Tsarevich, heir to the Russian throne, by George Dawe.

Siege of Sevastopol, from the Sevastopol Panorama Museum.

Coronation of Alexander II, by Mihaly Zichy, from Hermitage Museum.

Imam Shamil, leader of Muslim anti-Russian tribes in the Caucasus region.

The Battle of Shipka Pass in the Russo-Turkish War,
from the Plevna Panorama Museum.

*The Battle of Grivitsa Redoubt in the Russo-Turkish War,
from the Plevna Panorama Museum.*

The surrender of Osman Pasha to Alexander II in the Russo-Turkish War, 1877-78.

Alexander II in 1881, with his setter, Milord, by Konstantin Makovsky.

Serfs listening to the Emancipation Manifesto. Painting by Grigoriy Meyasoyedov.

Eleven: An End to Slavery

By 1860 only two ostensibly majority Christian, civilized, modern nations in the world still relegated certain people to the status of chattel, or slaves: the dictatorship of Russia and the democracy of the United States.

America's population of 31.5 million included 4 million slaves. In Russia, with a total population of 62.5 million, upwards of 50 million were serfs. About half were privately owned. The rest were property of the state.

The institution of serfdom died quietly in most of Europe as mechanization rendered it uneconomic and shifting morality found it reprehensible. It languished longer in Central Europe than in England or France, but was finally eliminated in Prussia and Austria by the Revolutions of 1848. The fact that it continued in Russia drew contempt from the rest of the Western world.

A small number of serfs were house servants or involved in manufacturing or transportation. Most were used for agriculture and were the property of those who owned the land on which they lived. The owners worked them like horses, except that horses sometimes lived and labored under better conditions than the two-legged livestock.

Serfs were restricted to the estates of their owners, without the right to travel or move to another master in search of better treatment or opportunities. They could not marry without the permission of their owners. The master could beat them with impunity, use them as collateral, sell them, gamble them away, break up families, have sex with the girls and women and add any offspring to his collection of forced laborers.

Discussions about granting freedom to the serfs had taken place under Catherine the Great and bubbled up from time to time among her successors. But it remained only talk. Minor reforms intended to ease the lot of the peasants were not enforced. The rulers were leery about bringing it up because whenever a rumor of possible emancipation reached the serfs themselves, as it did in 1796, it set off surges of unrest.

The government tracked these "disorders" closely. There was an average of 50 per year between 1796 and 1826. During the reign of Nicholas that average rose to 600 per year.

On coming to the throne, Alexander made ending serfdom his first priority. In March of 1856 he revealed his intention in a speech to an assembly of nobles.

"The present order of owning souls cannot remain unchanged," he said. "It is better to abolish serfdom from above than to wait for that time when it starts to abolish itself from below."

Defusing what the secret police had called "a keg of gunpowder" was not as simple as issuing an imperial edict. Emancipation would upset the entire labor system of the country. Though some landowners were prepared to rearrange their operations, most could be expected to oppose it.

For those objectors Alexander held a trump card. Many landowners had gone into debt trying to crank out a profit with the antiquated system. They turned to the crown to bail them out. By 1860 one-third of the estates and two-thirds of privately-owned serfs were mortgaged to the state or to banks connected to the royal family. They had no choice but to accept the Tsar's plan.

The impact of emancipation on the army presented a more complicated problem. Russia's military survival depended on the serfs. They filled its lower ranks and provided the cannon fodder. When poor weapons or bad strategy should have doomed the Russian army, enemies could still be defeated by the sheer size of the Tsar's forces, waves that came at them with many times more troops than they could possibly kill.

The million man army depended on a draft, but only serfs were drafted. Their enlistments were 25 years, a life sentence. Some peasant boys looked forward to dependable meals, good shelter and better clothing than their fellow villagers had, not to mention the opportunity to travel and, in times of peace, get more sleep than they could expect as field hands.

But for families who lost the strong arms of a male worker, conscription of a son was a terrible calamity.

Whether Alexander felt pangs of conscience about this inequality, he knew that a slave army was no match for one composed of men who, at some level, felt themselves freeborn, with individual rights and assets worth fighting for.

For five years he struggled over how the serfs could be given liberty without creating turmoil. More than 1,300 landowners met in 47 committees to wrangle over the details. The process was overseen by Alexander's liberal brother Konstantin who slowly but thoroughly saw to it that the Tsar's will — and his own — was done.

The Emancipation Manifesto ending serfdom was finally announced on February 19, 1861.

Russian elites who considered themselves liberals rejoiced. Governments around Europe sent their formal, and largely sincere, congratulations. The small but influential circle of expatriate Russians who had been lambasting the Tsar from outside the country showered their praise. The exiled writer Alexander Herzen, who published anti-Tsarist periodicals from the safety of London, wrote, "Neither the Russian people nor history will forget him for this. We hail him with the name 'Liberator.'"

Herzen was right. Of all the achievements of Alexander II, he remains best known as the man who freed the serfs. Alexander the Emancipator. Alexander the Liberator.

But as is so often the case with momentous acts undertaken with the best intentions, Alexander's liberation did not go as smoothly as hoped.

Twelve: The Frustrations of Freedom

Abraham Lincoln's Emancipation Proclamation, written as an executive order in the heat of a war, contained about 700 words and left little room for interpretation. Alexander's Emancipation Manifesto was accompanied by 17 separate acts and presented as agricultural reform legislation running more than 300 pages. There seems to be an immutable rule that the greater the number of words in any law, the less likely that law is to achieve its desired effect.

Though the Manifesto gave the serfs freedom, the right to marry, to own property and businesses, specifics differed depending on region and the status of a serf at the time of the emancipation. Serfs on private estates were immediately "freed" yet required to supply their former masters with an additional two years of labor. Those on state-owned lands would wait until 1866 for their freedom.

Serfs who worked on farms could obtain their own parcels of land provided they paid for them. Those with no money might receive a "pauper's allotment," a quarter of the land they had previously worked for themselves. House servants or serfs in factory work got nothing except their liberty.

The problems of the emancipation stemmed almost entirely from anger over how the land was distributed. Though both Russian serfs and American slaves were considered property, there were important differences between the two institutions.

Slaves had been kidnapped, ripped from their homelands and inserted into an alien environment, stripped of all family and community support.

Serfs, on the other hand, were surrounded by relatives and extended families. An ingrained cycle of customs and practices had been handed down in an unbroken chain of tradition that reached back 1,000 years or more. They had been working their native soil long before the latest batch of overlords appeared. They saw themselves as part of the dirt on which they had been born. "Our backs belong to the masters," went the saying. "But the land is ours."

In some ways they resembled sharecroppers more than slaves. Depending on the dictates of each owner, they performed a set amount of labor on the main estate — three days a week, sometimes more — and were allowed to use smaller individual plots from which they eked out food for their own use or, with permission of the master, for market.

They docilely submitted to a level of physical brutality that few of those reading this book could survive. They accepted the rapes of their wives, conscription of their sons and sale of their daughters.

But in matters of life or death, a famine for example, they were not above rebelling. Why should a starving man fear being shot? Killing a serf meant permanently depriving the owner of his property. It was a poor business practice, like a fisherman burning his boat. So for the most part, when a disorder broke out, all the rulers could do was whip their workers, which they did anyway.

In the best circumstances serfs saw the estate owner as being necessary to the well-ordered running of the estate on which they all depended for their lives. Overseers often left communal decisions, like settling minor disputes among villagers, to councils of elders.

Alexander's legislation gave official standing and greater powers to these traditional councils and codified their status. The landowners, of course, found ways to manipulate the law and used the councils to control the peasantry.

Among the decisions placed in the hands of the councils was what crops to plant and when to harvest. A rotation system that went back before memory usually left one third of the land to sit fallow each year. Peasants were thought to know how best to manage that.

It was a prehistoric and inefficient system. Planters in America and farmers in Europe were applying science to their crops and producing unprecedented yields. But when Russian estate owners wanted to increase profits they could only try to push their overworked serfs harder. That approach backfired more often than it succeeded. Like any beast of burden, the Russian peasant, the muscle of the state, could only be pushed so far.

Many of them felt they were pushed too far by the terms of the emancipation. In village after village they listened to the long reading of the manifesto with bewilderment, skepticism and doubt. They did not like what they heard.

Freedom was all well and good, but no one wanted to pay for land they saw as their patrimony, land worked by their fathers and grandfathers and bequeathed to their descendants. They did not like paying a higher than market value price for that land or being saddled with loans that obligated them to make payments to the government into the next century. They didn't like the fact that the masters, who retained half of the land, got first choice, taking the best soil and blocking off access to forests and other resources. They protested that the parcels left to them were too small to sustain their families.

Steeped in an almost mystical conception of the Tsar, they could not believe that their Father and Liberator intended such things. Rumors spread that the real manifesto gave them their land outright, that evil officials were hiding the truth, trying to deceive and steal from both the serfs and the Tsar.

Trouble was not long in coming. Two months after the manifesto was published, a literate peasant in the village of Bezdna announced that he had a copy of the true proclamation and, indeed, he said, the Tsar had commanded that all land be given to the serfs free of charge — just as everyone suspected. Thousands came to the village to hear the truth they wanted to hear. Soldiers followed and killed 400 in the crowd. More protests took place. The army responded with more bullets.

Things did not settle down until it became imperative to get the spring crop planted. The serfs returned to the fields to toil in the mud with their shovels and hoes as they always had, preparing the ancestral soil that they prayed would sustain their lives for one more year.

Freedom was an option. Food was not.

Thirteen: A Tentative Offer

In 1832 President Andrew Jackson sent his political crony James Buchanan to St. Petersburg as the American minister to Russia. Nicholas did not like republics or any whiff of democracy, but he embraced Buchanan who found the Tsar charming, "a man without moral blemish."

The ambassador, of course, was more interested in securing diplomatic advantages for his new and vulnerable nation than he was in moral blemishes. Likewise, Nicholas cared more about getting the upper hand on other monarchies in his sphere of influence than he did about a strange little country in a remote place that posed no danger to him.

The two nations actually had much they could agree on. American ships were increasingly carrying goods to and from Russian ports. Both preferred neutrality to alliances. And both detested the mighty British Empire.

Twelve years later America and England butted heads over the western part of North America. The British, having triumphed over China in the Opium War, began to think of the North Pacific as their lake. To that end, they were asserting their position in Oregon, California and the part of Canada now known as British Columbia.

There were few Americans in those regions, but the nation as a whole saw the territory as a natural part of their "manifest destiny." In 1844 James Polk ran for and won the presidency with the slogan "Fifty-four Forty or Fight!," promoting the proposition that the United States' claims reached all the way to the southern tip of Russian America at latitude 54°40'. The British were resolved not to give up their claims as far as the 54th parallel. But they didn't want to fight either.

Buchanan, now Polk's Secretary of State, negotiated the Oregon Treaty of 1846, which separated British and American territories at

49°, the latitude set from Minnesota to Montana after the War of 1812. Neither side seemed happy about it.

Buchanan's next post took him to London where he was the U.S. ambassador in the run-up to the Crimean War. He happily shared information about Britain's military preparations with his old friend Nicholas.

America stood out as the only nation in the world that supported Russia in the conflict. Franklin Pierce, President from 1853 to 1857, seriously considered jumping into the fray. America sold ships to the Russian-American Company and supplied the colony with American-flagged ships that could not be attacked by the allies under the laws of war. Kentucky riflemen volunteered to fight the British in Crimea. American doctors went to Sevastopol to aid wounded Russians. American weapons, including a whole shipload of gunpowder, were sent to aid the defenders of Petropavlovsk.

It was at this time that the beleaguered Nicholas tentatively raised the possibility of selling Russian America to the United States. President Pierce, a fervent expansionist, was intrigued. In the preceding few years, America had acquired undisputed ownership of everything from the Mississippi River to California, Texas and Puget Sound. Outflanking the British with Alaska would make a nice addition. But domestic issues were Pierce's immediate concern, in particular whether to allow slavery in the nation's recently acquired territory.

Nicholas was in no hurry. He probably didn't want to part with one square inch of his empire and kept the discussions secret. The few advisors who knew anything about it didn't take the proposition seriously.

Except for one, Nikolay Muravyov, the conqueror of the Amur. With the Far East under firm Russian control, the nation no longer needed its precarious American outposts. Siberia was united by land routes. It could all be connected and supplied by railroads, without depending on vulnerable ships. Moreover, the California gold rush and the Oregon Treaty made America, not Britain, the new dominant power on the Pacific Coast.

"Sooner or later we shall have to surrender our North American possessions," Muravyov wrote in 1853. It would be best if those possessions were in the hands of a friendly United States rather than the British leviathan, he thought. The Americans could provide a cushion between Canada and Siberia.

Muravyov didn't say so, but he considered Russian America to be competition for his own plans in the Far East. Both American and Siberian authorities were constantly petitioning the government for assistance and money. A ruble spent on New Archangel meant one less ruble for Siberia. If the Tsar determined that Alaska was too valuable to give up, it would set back development of Muravyov's new city of Vladivostok.

Muravyov found an ally in Alexander's brother Konstantin, now in charge of the Russian Navy. Konstantin had the responsibility of connecting the sparsely-settled wilderness with ships that sailed halfway around the world at significant expense. Stockholders of the Russian-American Company didn't think the Tsar would be persuaded to abandon them. But those who agreed with Muravyov began to collect whatever negative information they could find or imagine regarding the colony to prepare their case.

James Buchanan became the American President in 1857. Quiet discussions about Alaska continued under the direction of Russia's Minister to the United States, Edouard de Stoeckl. Stoeckl had arrived in Washington as a low-level diplomat in 1841 and discovered he liked the place. He stayed in the country as he rose through the ranks and married an American belle, Elisa Howard.

Buchanan was well-disposed toward Russia, but he had his own powder keg about to explode. Friction between the states that abhorred slavery and those whose economies required it was reaching the boiling point. Settlers were killing each other in Kansas. An attempt to create a slave rebellion by anti-slave firebrand John Brown in 1859 ended with the deaths of U.S. soldiers and Brown's collaborators. The trial and execution of the rabid abolitionist ignited a public furor.

It is a tragic irony that Buchanan, one of the most accomplished international diplomats of his generation, was unable to save his own country from a bloodbath.

The American Civil War was already underway when Alexander announced his Emancipation Manifesto. Further talk of buying Alaska would need to be postponed while the world held its breath and waited to see whether North or South would prevail.

The great powers of Europe were inclined to sympathize with the Confederacy. The factories of Britain and France needed cheap cotton and no one wanted to see America get any stronger than it already was. Both governments planned to intervene if they saw fit.

Union forces held the advantage over the Confederacy in terms of manpower, manufacturing and money. But the threat of international support for the South loomed large. Union warships blockaded Southern ports and prevented contact with Europe. But if Britain were to decide to use its own navy, the biggest in the world, to keep trade open with the South, America would be helpless to stop it.

Secretary of State William Seward barely managed to keep the Europeans tentatively neutral. The whim of Emperor Napoleon III, who picked this moment to attempt the conquest of Mexico, or an abrupt change of government in England could force the United States to fight the most powerful nations on Earth in addition to the breakaway Confederacy.

In all of Europe only two countries officially supported the Union, the Papal States and Russia. Aid from the Pope was limited to moral approval, but Russia could do something physical.

In September of 1863 Russian warships appeared almost simultaneously in New York Harbor and San Francisco Bay. The "goodwill tour" had not been announced. American officials may have discussed it with their Russian associates, but it appears that no formal invitation was offered.

Nonetheless, the Americans rejoiced at the sight of their one friend coming to visit and bringing big guns with them. "Thank God for the Russians," wrote Gideon Welles, Lincoln's Secretary of the Navy.

The visit lasted seven months during which prominent Americans and curious common folk were welcomed on board. One tourist was the First Lady, Mary Todd Lincoln. Foreign governments who might have been thinking about sticking their noses into America's war reconsidered. When Alexander's fleet finally left American ports, the Union was well on its way to winning the conflict and Seward was satisfied that neither the British nor the French nor anyone else would assist the South.

The Russian courtesy call marked a high point in relations between the two countries. Alexander could feel proud of himself and his military.

But he could not feel at ease. He had his own insurrection to deal with inside his own realm.

Fourteen: The Polish Bloodbath

Russia's Empire included the Kingdom of Poland. The once sovereign county had been sliced up and passed around like a tray of cheese by Russia, Prussia and Austria since the 18th century. The Tsar ruled the greater part and had the title King of Poland. Any fig leaf of independence was plucked away when Nicholas sent 180,000 troops to stamp out an insurrection in 1831.

The Poles rightly considered the union a forced marriage. Among the differences between the states was the status of Poland's midlevel nobility, the szlachta. Early in the middle ages local warlords such as the barons of England held the reins of power. Kings answered to them. Then, as nation states developed, kings centralized their authority, becoming autocrats to whom nobles were subject.

Poland was an exception. The szlachta maintained and even expanded their individual rights to such an extent that the kings of Polish blood became little more than figureheads.

The szlachta considered themselves to have descended from the wild Asiatic tribes of antiquity. They liked to wear turbans and other Oriental-themed clothing, usually accompanied by a scimitar. Before the Reformation their numbers included Jews and even a few Muslims. Their holdings were often small, hardly enough to support their families and the serfs who depended on them. But being poor was not a mark against a member of the szlachta. Their nobility was in their blood and independence. Each felt as important as the next. Decisions about the nation were made by a congress of their members and had to be unanimous. Even one dissent was enough to stop any action.

As admirable as such a government might be in leading to a kind of middle class democracy, it was no way to protect a country surrounded by large and hungry enemies. Thus Poland became a vassal.

Yet the szlachta remained. They were exceedingly unhappy with Alexander's Emancipation Manifesto. Their dissatisfaction created an odd union between conservative landowners and the country's idealistic liberal intellectuals.

The Polish powder keg went off in August of 1861 as young men came together in ad hoc protests over being drafted into the Russian army. Martial law was declared. Public executions and deportations of protesters and their sympathizers only served to turn the demonstrations into a guerrilla war. A Polish provisional government formed with the goal of throwing off the Russian yoke.

Early in 1863 uprisings began almost simultaneously in the Russian part of Poland and adjacent lands, including the Ukraine, Belarus and Lithuania. Patriots looted armories and killed Russian officials on sight. An army of rebellion — actually several small, loosely coordinated units — took to the field and prevailed in a surprising number of encounters even though they were outnumbered ten to one.

The provisional government hoped that Britain would be as supportive of their cause as they had been of the Turks. Napoleon III of France made vague promises of assistance. But in the end the victors of the Crimean War offered nothing but sympathy.

Prussia, which held western Poland, sided with the Tsar. Chancellor Bismarck assisted with supplies and making his nation's railroads available for the transport of troops.

In an attempt to win over the peasantry, the provisional government granted land to Polish serfs. But in spite of this generosity, the serfs didn't particularly help either the Russians or the rebels.

The Polish resistance fought heroically. But for every Russian they killed two more took his place. By the end of 1864, after hundreds of battles and skirmishes and an estimated 25,000 Poles dead, the rebellion was over. Under Count Mikhail Muravyev, the general sent to restore order, entire towns were burned to the ground. Muravyev became known as "The Hangman."

Officially almost 400 people were executed and 20,000 men and women exiled to Siberia. Some historians put the number much higher, between 70,000 and 80,000, which would make it the biggest mass deportation in Russian history.

The power of the szlachta was shattered. In Poland 1,660 estates were confiscated along with an additional 1,794 in Lithuania. An income tax of 10 percent was placed on all estates to cover the cost of suppressing the rebellion. Whereas Russian serfs had to buy their land at an average cost one-third higher than market value, serfs in Poland were allowed to pay market value. Unlike in Russia, Polish house serfs were given land. And, although they could sell their land to another serf, no serf could sell his land to a member of the szlachta.

Under these favorable terms, it is estimated that, in the entire Russian Empire, 90 percent of the peasants who actually wound up owning land after the emancipation lived in Poland and adjacent territories.

Though it was intended to punish Poland's established middle and upper castes, Alexander's liberality to the Polish serfs succeeded in creating an increasingly well-off and well-educated working class.

But in a country where it was better to be noble than to be rich, such largesse could not buy loyalty. Within a generation the sons of the serfs liberated by the Tsar would be in open sympathy with the disenfranchised szlachta and another rebellion would start to simmer.

Poles still see Alexander as a monster drenched in the blood of innocent victims.

Things went very differently in the Grand Duchy of Finland. Like Poland, Finland was an integral part of the Empire, governed under a slightly alternate understanding, though with just as much repression.

Had the Finns revolted at the same time as the Poles, either or both might have succeeded in breaking free of Russia. But the Finns stayed out of it. They were more likely to think of themselves as part of the Tsar's realm than were the Poles. The typical Pole was oriented toward Western Europe. A Finn was more willing to travel within the vast Empire and serve it.

For example, aside from Cossacks and a few indigenous people from East Asia, the primary settlers in Russian America were Finnish. The first missionaries to the colony came from a monastery in Finland. Finnish boatwrights and carpenters plied their trade in Kodiak and New Archangel. Finnish Lutherans had the only non-Orthodox church allowed in the colony. As late as 1959, the year Alaska became a state, the sailing ship *Trader*, built by Finns in Russian America, carried freight between villages on the lower Yukon River.

Even after Alaska became American property, Saami, or Laplanders, traveled to the New World to teach Native Alaskans the skill of reindeer herding. Their descendants still live throughout the state. They include Margie Brown, former CEO of Cook Inlet Region Inc., one of the wealthiest corporations in Alaska. A reunion of Alaska Saami families held in Poulsbo, Washington in 1998 drew more than 150 people.

Alexander was grateful for the loyalty of the Finns during the Crimean War. It was time to reward them and, not coincidentally, to remove a possible cause for further trouble. In 1863, as his army was executing Polish rebels, civilians and priests, Alexander convoked the Finnish national assembly, the Diet, which had been disbanded in 1809 and had never reconvened in the intervening years.

The relationship went smoothly. The representatives in the Diet behaved cautiously but responsibly and the citizens followed their lead. In 1869 Alexander took the next step and confirmed a constitution for the Duchy. This may seem like an obvious progression, but nowhere else in Russia did a written contract exist between the government and the governed.

The Tsar was still the head of Finland with the title of Grand Duke. But whereas he was a dictator in Poland, in Finland he was something brand new in the history of Russian rulers, a constitutional monarch.

In 1894, the Finns installed a fine statue of Alexander in the middle of Senate Square at the heart of Helsinki. It stands there today. The Government House is on his right hand, Helsinki University on his left. Behind him rise the lofty domes of Helsinki Cathedral. When Alexander's successors resumed repressing Finland the public protested by bringing flowers to the statue of "The Good Tsar."

Finland is one place where Alexander is still called "The Liberator."

Fifteen: The Price of Reform

The emancipation of the serfs has overshadowed other reforms instituted by Alexander. They were many.

Alexander relaxed the stranglehold on speech and writing that marked his father's rule. Russians were allowed to travel abroad. University admission was opened to more classes of society. Foreigners were granted civil rights. Jews with scholarly degrees or a craft or who had completed their military service were free to settle where they wished and allowed to serve in the government.

Expanding freedom of the press worked in Alexander's favor at first. Newspapers praised the emancipation of the serfs. In the Polish crisis they roused public opinion against the rebels.

But inevitably voices arose questioning or objecting to imperial decisions. This typically took place obliquely. Writers accused a subordinate of not doing as the Tsar wished, even though everyone knew the subordinate was only following orders.

Nonetheless, Alexander kept a loose rein on the press compared to his predecessor. Rather than prohibit specific statements in advance and clear every word prior to publication, he waited for the writing to be printed. At that point, if anything intolerable was found, a journal might be closed down for weeks or perhaps forever. In extreme cases some writers were imprisoned. By and large the Russian press corps figured out what its boundaries were and made a specialty of writing to the edge without stepping over.

With the Crimean War in mind, Alexander set out to reform the military. The troops in Sevastopol had consisted of serfs and criminals, often treated more viciously by their own abusive officers than they might have expected to be had they fallen into the hands of the opposing armies.

As Tsarevich, Alexander had watched soldiers beat a comrade to death in the course of punishing him for violating some rule. As Tsar, he made discipline more humane. He banned corporal punishment and branding. The practice of restricting the draft to serfs ended and universal conscription for all ranks of society was instituted. He drastically shortened the term of service and made exceptions for men with compelling family obligations. Conscripts received a basic education. The military became the most egalitarian institution in Russia.

He rewrote Russia's jumble of laws and reorganized the justice system. Trials had been secret, verdicts connected more to bribes than to evidence. Endless appeals kept decisions dangling for decades.

Alexander's judicial reforms were, if anything, more sweeping than his abolition of serfdom. Cases were now settled by juries with able advocates arguing opposing sides. Their stirring speeches and summaries were printed in the liberated press.

In addition, Alexander took the unprecedented step of publishing the national budget. For the first time in history, Russians could see how the government was spending its money.

He revamped the Orthodox Church, opening seminaries to students whether they were related to clergy or not, abolishing the clerical caste and reorganizing parishes.

His father had maintained a highly centralized government in which the Tsar's approval was needed for every decision, no matter how small. Under Alexander, local affairs were put in the hands of district assemblies. These represented the landed gentry and were responsible for keeping roads and bridges in order, paying for education and sanitation, tracking crops and keeping a watch out for the possibility of famine.

The years that immediately followed the emancipation were largely prosperous ones, in some cases spectacularly so. Russia had only one railroad and 570 miles of track in 1855. By 1880 there were 14,000 miles of track and the western part of the nation was communicating by telegraph.

In 1861 there were 2,238 private companies in the whole country. By 1887 there were more than ten times that many. In 1861 Russia had 78 joint stock companies with an estimated value of 72 million rubles. Twelve years later there were 357 such entities with a total value of more than one billion rubles.

More people were getting rich in Russia than had ever happened before and the wealth was more evenly distributed. But intense poverty continued to be the lot of most Russians. The poor themselves didn't grumble about it so much. They were used to being destitute and overworked. But another group of people, not so destitute and unaccustomed to any kind of physical work, looked at the inequity and insisted that it must end.

This was a new generation, young people who did not remember the suppression of Nicholas' time. They read novels and treatises and newspapers that could not have seen print 30 years earlier. They were aware of developments in Europe — democracy, socialism, communism — and wondered why no one else could see how wonderful these developments would be for Russia's lower classes.

More than a few felt certain that, reforms aside, nothing was going to change for them. Nothing big. Although advancement in the bureaucracy or business was more open than it had been, it remained limited to the very few.

These young people met and talked. They petitioned when they thought it might do some good. It didn't. Any improvement would have to come from the top, as it always had in Russia. Some muttered that for true progress to occur, the top had to be removed.

On April 4, 1866, Alexander took his customary afternoon walk in a garden a short carriage ride from the Winter Palace in St. Petersburg. He did this every day. Crowds always gathered to get a look at him. As he was about to get back in the carriage a gunshot rang out.

An expelled University of Moscow student named Dmitry Karakozov was caught. He was a nobleman involved with a small, secret group dedicated to the proposition that killing the Tsar would cause the masses to rise in revolt and throw off their masters, opening the way to a new society of equality and brotherhood.

The secret police quickly discovered and arrested Karakozov's associates. The gunman was sentenced to death along with his cousin, Nikolai Ishutin, who had organized the group of which Karakozov was a member and instructed the would-be assassin. Karakozov begged the Tsar for his life, but was hanged. At the last moment Ishutin's sentence was commuted to hard labor in Siberia.

Alexander was shaken. While other Tsars had been murdered by those wishing to take their place, Karakozov acted on a previously unimagined impulse. He had not shot in order to become the next Tsar, but to end Tsardom itself.

Count Muravyev, "The Hangman," was brought out of retirement to lead the investigation into possible collaborators. He suspected everyone. Princes, peasants, students, teachers, merchants and military officers. Russia shuddered in expectation of a return to tyranny.

Muravyev died before the year was out. Over the protests of Konstantin and other liberals, Peter Shuvalov, a more sophisticated but equally ruthless officer, became the new chief of the secret police. He would stay in power as the Tsar's right hand man for eight years, prime minister in all but name. The reforms would come to a halt and, in some cases, be reversed.

Grand Duke Konstantin still had Alexander's ear and affection. But the Tsar had concluded that his reforms had gone too far. His little brother knew much about politics and naval warfare and remained his primary advisor concerning Russian America.

But Konstantin could not see things with the clarity of a man who had just been missed by a bullet.

Sixteen: Grief and Love

Tsarevich Alexander, later Alexander III,
with bride-elect Princess Dagmar of Denmark, later Tsarina Maria Fyodorovna.

A different kind of bullet had already pierced Alexander's heart. His oldest son and heir, Nicholas Alexandrovich, died of tuberculosis of the spine in April of 1865.

The disease set in following an injury in an impromptu wrestling match with his cousin. He had been sent to Nice for treatment. Doctors soon sent word that death was at hand. Traveling by train, the royal family reached him in three days, faster than anyone had ever made such a trip. En route they picked up the Princess of Denmark, Dagmar, young Nicholas' fiancée. Together the parents and bride-elect surrounded his bed, weeping and holding hands as the Tsarevich passed away.

Nicholas had been considered by all and one to be the hope of Russia's future, intelligent, decisive, personable, handsome and athletic.

The heir apparent was now the next oldest son. Alexander Alexandrovich was everything his brother was not. He was large, slow, clumsy, something of a self-deprecating clown. He was said to be kind. He was not said to be smart. Instead of studying the arts required of a ruler he had satisfied himself — with his father's approval — with showy uniforms and parades.

He would become Tsar Alexander III. He also became the spouse of Princess Dagmar. It was perhaps as close as either of them could come in this life to being near the departed man they both adored.

Shortly after Nicholas' death, the last gun was fired in America's Civil War. It happened months after Confederate General Robert E. Lee surrendered his army at Appomattox. And it happened in Russian waters.

The Confederate raider *Shenandoah* trapped a Yankee whaling fleet near the Arctic Circle in June of 1865, capturing 21 vessels in the course of a few hours and sinking most of them. It would be another month before the Confederate captain received certain news from a passing British vessel that the war was over, something his frantic captives had tried to tell him as he torched their ships and valuable whale oil in the ice off Alaska.

If the tiny Confederate Navy could put a warship between Russia and her colony, what might the much bigger U.S. Navy do? The question of Russian America could no longer be avoided.

With his beloved son dead, cannon fire off his eastern coast and a close brush with an assassin's bullet, Alexander might be excused for feeling gloomy and ruminating on the futility of trying to do good and difficult things to help people who did not care.

Then a third bullet struck. This one, however, brought him more joy than anything else he would ever experience.

He had been enamored of Ekaterina Dolgorusky since he first laid eyes on her. She was 12 and he was 40. When she was 16 she came to Moscow and was received at court. Alexander was never good at hiding his emotions and everyone could see he was smitten.

It was no great thing for a young lady of good breeding to spend time in the Tsar's bed. It happened all the time. In some ways it was a stepping stone to a profitable marriage to a rich old man somewhere in the country, which is where the girls tended to be sent when the Tsar grew bored with them after a few days or hours.

This did not happen with Ekaterina. Instead she and Alexander entered into a chaste, platonic affair. They met and talked. Just talked. They took walks with his favorite setter, Milord, running in front of them. Her family and sponsors began to worry that she would never reap the rewards that came from sleeping with the Tsar, rewards they hoped would benefit themselves.

But platonic love can go only so far. She comforted him with sympathy when Nicholas died. She bestowed a few joyful kisses behind a tree when he survived the assassination attempt.

In July 1866 they finally made love in a small out-of-the-way palace used by previous Tsars for their assignations. He is said to have told her, "You are my secret wife. If I am ever free, I will marry you."

He was as good as his word. But the words of others made her cringe. The court rumbled with rumors. Everyone knew Alexander was having sex with the girl. But no one could know, she could not tell them, how much they truly loved each other. It was agony for both of them.

To escape, she made a visit to Italy. An alternate tale was deliberately circulated, that the Tsar had grown bored with this one, too, and she was gone. Court gossips moved on to other victims.

Alexander wrote her every day. The absence was more than he could stand. As 1867 dawned he had two great secrets to keep from the Russian public. One was Ekaterina.

The other was what he planned to do about Russian America.

Seventeen: Farewell to America

*Grand Duke Konstantin, younger brother of Alexander II,
who insisted the Tsar sell Russian America.*

The first telegraph messages between Europe and America by underwater cable were exchanged in 1858. It was a slow and trouble-plagued system, but it signaled that a new era of rapid global communications had commenced.

Many hoped the invention would end wars. How could people who talked to each other ever fight? Replying to the first congratulatory telegram sent from Queen Victoria — 98 words that took 16 hours to decode — President Buchanan called the invention "a triumph more glorious, because far more useful to mankind, than was ever won by conqueror on the field of battle … a bond of perpetual peace and friendship between the kindred nations."

Public celebrations took place in New York and London. Journalists and essayists sang the praises of the modern miracle. Within a few years Hans Christian Andersen wrote a children's story about it and American poet John Greenleaf Whittier wrote a long, beautiful ode honoring it.

By the fall of 1866 a second and a much improved cable was in place. It could transmit eight words a minute, still slow, but fast enough to make useful regular connections between transoceanic governments. This technological breakthrough would have much to do with what happened to Alaska the following year.

A telegraph through Russian America had been touted as an alternative to the original, problematic Atlantic line. With the blessing and endorsement of Secretary of State Seward, the Western Union company proposed an overland route through Canada and down the Yukon River connecting to Siberia with a short cable under the Bering Strait. American survey crews were at work in western Alaska when word reached them of the upgraded oceanic cable that made their project superfluous. It looked like American interests in Alaska were fated to pack up and go home.

Russians saw their New World colony as a distant yet integral part of the Empire. Geography books noted it briefly, but with exciting illustrations and a note of pride. "Our Russia," a children's board game, included Alaska. The extravagant Russian Ethnographic Exhibition held in Moscow in early 1867 featured detailed representations of Native Alaskans among the 300 mannequins in regional costumes, accompanied by goods and artifacts from their areas and arrayed to demonstrate the intercontinental expanse of the multi-ethnic nation.

Meanwhile, Alexander and his councilors were discussing whether to relinquish the colony and, if so, under what terms. America had seemed receptive prior to the Civil War and it was generally agreed that the United States would be a good neighbor, disinclined to expand across to Asia and protective of Russia's back door.

But the Civil War had changed things. America had lost much blood and treasure. Many citizens had their hands full tending to affairs at home. America's merchant fleet had been crippled — not so much because of the hulls sunk by Confederate raiders, for those could be replaced, but by the steep insurance rates placed on American ships during the war by British companies that controlled the market. Those rates put many Yankee shippers out of business and forced them to sell their fleets at ruinously low prices. The English stood ready to buy everything afloat at pennies on the dollar. As a result, Britannia continued to rule the waves for another half century.

To further complicate matters, a policy devised by Secretary of State Seward had backfired and aroused Canada from placidity. Seward had attempted an economic boycott of the provinces hoping to force them into joining the United States. It had the opposite effect. The Canadians stoically endured the boycott. They tightened both their belts and their ties with the mother country. By 1867 the huge region north of the 49th parallel was preparing to unite in a confederation.

The British government, which had long resisted such a separate status for Canada, now encouraged it. America was tired of war, but it possessed the most modern and seasoned armed force in the world, an army bigger than any except Russia's and bristling with new, precise giant guns and rapid-fire rifles, all concentrated a few days' march from 90 percent of Canada's small population. Compared to conquering the South, Canada would be a relatively easy capture. The British reasoned that democratic America would be less inclined to attack another independent democracy than they would be to attack a colony. The Dominion of Canada would be such a country.

Finally, relations between Britain and Russia had eased since the Crimean War. Under the circumstances there seemed to be no reason to hand the colony to America, assuming America was still interested.

Governor Muravyov had left for retirement in Paris urging Alexander to get rid of the North American colony and focus on the Far East. The Tsar's brother Konstantin took up the cause. He argued that Alaska Natives were receiving brutal treatment at the hands of the Russian-American Company, that the company was violating laissez-faire practices by imposing arbitrary and overreaching rules, and that the company's finances were criminally mismanaged, costing the crown money that would better be spent elsewhere.

A commission was formed to travel to the colony and report back on the situation. Briefed by Konstantin, the commissioners expected the worst.

Instead they found the company making a profit, its books in good order. The "overreaching" rules, such as those that limited the taking of sea otter and seal, were necessary to preserve the animals for the future. And though there was horrific truth to the tales of abuse of Native Americans in the past, by 1860 that was old history. Indigenous people who lived in proximity to Russians were not slaves;

if anything they were better treated than Indians in the United States. Their assistance was more necessary to the survival and prosperity of the tiny Russian colony than was the case with settlements on the Great Plains, the Pacific coast or the wild West.

Young Aleut and Tlingit men studied commerce, shipbuilding and other sciences at universities in St. Petersburg and Moscow. A creole class had arisen through intermarriage, an educated group who were fluent and literate in both their aboriginal language and Russian, aware of the traditions and needs of their relatives but faithful members of the Orthodox Church and loyal to the Tsar. They were recognized as the solid foundation of an emerging Russian American bourgeois class.

Without a good reason to do otherwise, Alexander approved a directive in 1866 that would extend for 20 years the Russian-American Company's charter to control all commercial activities in Alaska. It seemed like the final word. But Konstantin was persistent in asking the Tsar to reconsider.

Stoeckl was recalled from the United States for consultations. He had done splendidly in his American years and was due for a promotion to a prestigious office at The Hague. He was convinced that America would soon acquire Canada and would logically want Alaska, too.

On everyone's mind was the matter of Russia's finances. The imperial treasury faced a debt that required the country to seek millions of dollars in foreign loans. Alexander, already planning to take military revenge for the Crimean War, did not want to be in debt to anyone. If the Americans were willing to part with cold, hard cash, perhaps he could see his way to giving up an expendable part of his real estate.

Prince Alexander Gorchakov, the Foreign Minister, aligned with the conservative faction and resisted the change. He was aware of the latent resources in the colony and the potential geographical advantage it could offer in the future. He advised Stoeckl to keep talking to the Americans, but not to act too quickly. He insisted that the Tsar should not accept a cent less than $5 million for it.

Stoeckl returned to Washington, not happy about having to postpone his advancement to The Hague and anxious to complete the business he had pursued for 15 years.

He arrived in New York in February of 1867 and immediately sent a message to Seward informing the Secretary of State that he was back on an urgent mission regarding Russian America.

The time had come for serious talk.

Eighteen: A Deal in the Night

Eduard de Stoeckl, Russia's minister to the U.S. who signed the papers selling Alaska, from Library of Congress, Prints and Photographs Division.

Seward may have wondered which issues regarding Russian America Stoeckl had in mind. There were several on his desk at the moment, mostly involving access to resources and trade. But he would have to wait to find out. Stoeckl took ill almost as soon as he got off the ship and was out of commission for nearly a month.

As soon as he was able, he met with Seward at the State Department. The Secretary first inquired whether people in Washington state might be granted fishing rights in Alaska. Probably not, Stoeckl replied. The Russians had always resisted foreign ships in their waters.

Seward cut to the chase. Would Russia be willing to sell the colony?

Make an offer, Stoeckl said.

The Secretary's heart leapt. For years the enticing prospect of acquiring Russian America had been thwarted by Russian coyness, international concerns and the War between the States. It had been like a long, slow card game in which each player acted like they really weren't interested.

Now the Tsar was calling America's hand.

William Henry Seward was born in 1801, when the United States stopped at the Mississippi River. He proved to be a brilliant student and went on to a career as a prosperous lawyer, Governor of New York and U.S. Senator. He had been considered the likely Republican nominee for the presidential election of 1860 and was flabbergasted when the nomination went to Abraham Lincoln instead. But he campaigned energetically for the candidate from Illinois and, upon Lincoln's election, was chosen to serve as Secretary of State.

In Lincoln's Cabinet his main job was to keep other countries from meddling with the Union's efforts to subdue the South. He became Lincoln's closest confidant, counseling him on domestic as well as foreign matters. Savvy in the ways of Washington, Lincoln counted on him to help pass needed legislation, often in the face of bitter opposition. A foe of slavery, Seward was credited as the editor, if not the co-author, of the Emancipation Proclamation.

On the night that Lincoln was killed, one of assassin John Wilkes Booth's collaborators attacked Seward with a knife, stabbing him repeatedly in the face, chest and neck. He survived and continued in his post at the State Department after Vice President Andrew Johnson succeeded Lincoln.

Like most Americans of his generation, Seward was a fervent believer in the idea of manifest destiny, the inevitable expansion of the United States to the Pacific Ocean and beyond. American citizens rejoiced to see their map extended to include the Western prairies, the Rocky Mountains, Texas, California and the Pacific Northwest.

But Seward knew there was more than national pride at stake. The destruction of the Yankee arctic whaling fleet by the *Shenandoah* had dealt a significant economic blow to America's maritime interests. Even more frustrating was the fact that the Confederate raider managed to evade the mighty U.S. Navy. The *Shenandoah*'s race across two oceans to reach the safe haven of Liverpool, England remains one of the most spectacular nautical exploits of all time.

The *Shenandoah* showed that the United States needed more ports on the West Coast if it wanted to dominate the Pacific. Those ports were in Alaska and lay close to the Great Circle Route, the shortest distance between California and the Orient.

Seward moved quickly to get President Johnson's approval and began working out a contract with Stoeckl. By mid-March they had an agreement. The territory would be purchased for $7 million with an additional $200,000 to settle any civil claims that might arise.

Seward presented the plan to Johnson's Cabinet, which unanimously approved it on March 19, 1867. Stoeckl cabled the contract to St. Petersburg where it was presented to Alexander. Satisfied that the document was sufficient, and perhaps delighted that the sale was bringing in $2 million more than he'd expected, Alexander consented on March 26.

Stoeckl received the telegram with the Tsar's orders late on March 29. He called at Seward's house to tell him the news. It was approaching midnight, but the Secretary was known to be a night owl, a lover of theater, sponsor of lavish parties and, on a typical evening, likely to be found playing cards and smoking cigars until the wee hours.

He was engaged in a game of whist when the Russian minister was shown in. "Tomorrow, if you like, I will come to your department and we can enter upon the treaty," Stoeckl said.

Seward set down his cards and pushed the table away. "Why wait until tomorrow, Baron?" he said. "Let us make the treaty tonight."

Stoeckl was caught off guard. The clerks needed to prepare the paperwork would be home and probably in bed.

Nonsense, Seward insisted. The State Department will be open for business at midnight. My staff and I will be waiting for you.

By 4 a.m. the documents were signed and sealed and ready to be sent to the President.

Seward had powerful incentives to finish the transaction quickly. It would require the approval of Congress, which was set to adjourn soon. And the political ground was crumbling under him. The Cabinet Johnson inherited from Lincoln showed every sign of disintegrating in rancor. It could shatter at any moment and sink the Alaska matter once again, perhaps for good.

Finally, Seward felt it was imperative to let the British and Canadians know right away that Alaska was America's. The

Washington newspapers would have the story by the next day and the London papers a few hours later.

But there was no statement from the Tsar or his Foreign Office. The Russian newspapers and the Russian public learned about it from the reports that originated across the ocean.

The reaction in Russia was one of overwhelming consternation. The Russian-American Company had no advance warning that it was about to go out of business. The Orthodox Church protested at the "sale" of its flock. Admiral Vasily Zavoyko, an officer with the Russian-American Company, the man who had led the valiant defense of Petropavlovsk during the Crimean War, adamantly and publicly refused to sign papers acknowledging the Tsar's action. He was demoted, forcibly retired and exiled from St. Petersburg. The Russian press widely condemned the sale in such angry terms that the government threatened to bring charges of sedition.

Such threats silenced those disappointed at losing the colony. But American historian Hector Chevigny writes that throughout Russia a feeling of national shame and guilt set in that continues to the present day.

The Tsar never explained himself. Instead, he let his messenger take the punishment. Stoeckl would not go to The Hague. He received no further assignments but was pensioned off and retired, an unperson.

Chevigny notes, "The wish to forget him is evident in the failure of Russian reference works even to mention his name."

Nineteen: Assault in Paris

Selling Russia America with all its space and promise strikes present-day Alaskans as shortsighted and callous. But Alexander's attitude toward the colony is echoed by many modern scholars. British historian Geoffrey Hosking dismisses Russia's adventure in America in a sentence, saying it achieved "only the sparsest of settlement and never put down roots."

Whether the decision was smart or dumb, the Tsar had other things on his mind in the spring of 1867. His one-time adversary, Napoleon III, had rebuilt Paris and was showing off his City of Lights in a glorious world's fair, the International Exposition. It would bring exhibitions from nations as far away as Japan in a showcase of international culture and the latest scientific advances. World leaders would be stopping by to see and be seen.

The French Emperor was eager to befriend the Tsar. In the aftermath of the Crimean War France had suffered embarrassing setbacks in Mexico and Italy. Meanwhile, Alexander's uncle, King William of Prussia, and his right hand man, Bismarck, were turning Germany into a major world power, absorbing surrounding territory and building armed might.

Alexander might have felt smug when the German troops defeated Austria, the presumed friend that had turned on Russia during the Crimean crisis. But he and Napoleon III both knew that they had a serious potential enemy in Prussia.

When Alexander decided to attend the world's fair no one thought anything special about it. This was exactly the kind of high-profile festivity where the world would expect a great ruler to show up and hobnob with other great rulers.

What no one knew, not even his own secret police, was that Alexander didn't give a hoot about hobnobbing. Ekaterina would be there, waiting for him in the privacy of an anonymous mansion.

The imperial delegation stayed at the Élysée Palace. Alexander slipped out at midnight and didn't return until after dawn. His retinue fell into a state of panic, unable to understand why he had disappeared without telling anyone. The city was full of Polish refugees. Shouts of "Long live Poland!" had taunted the Russians when they arrived. Any one of these angry people might try to strike him.

Alexander dismissed their worries. In the weeks that followed a cab brought Ekaterina to the Élysée Palace every night. He was the happiest man in Paris. The happiest man in Europe. In the company of the happiest men who had ever lived.

By day the Tsar and his son toured the marvelous exhibits and attended festivities with other heads of state. He was returning from a military review in an open carriage with Napoleon III when two shots rang out at close range.

Anton Berezovski, a 20-year-old Pole, was targeting Alexander, but he had bad aim. He was arrested on the spot and confessed to the crime. Reports in the French newspapers were not what the Tsar expected. Writers blamed the royal victim and praised the courage and principles of the freedom-fighting, patriotic Polish shooter.

Alexander coolly completed his visit to show he was not afraid of such malcontent trash. The French justice system, he was confident, would sentence the man to death.

Instead, after a trial in which the defense accused the Tsar of tyrannical cruelty, Berezovski received a life sentence with a good chance at early parole. Napoleon III sent a specially-made bullet-proof carriage to Alexander in St. Peterburg, either as something of an apology or something of a grim joke between despots in the form of a gift. The Tsar accepted the carriage, but could no longer trust France.

Bismarck instantly understood what the assassination attempt meant for his grand strategy. It meant Alexander would not hurry to assist Napoleon III. Prussia's eastern border would be safe when the time came to attack France on the west.

In 1870 Prussia did just that, destroying the French military overnight. Napoleon III pleaded with Russia to help, but no aid came. He was captured and ingloriously packed off to live out his final years in England. In a stroke, Bismarck's German Empire had become a European superpower with national goals that would dominate history for the next 75 years.

Berezovski's bullets had one other significant effect. They caused the Tsar to bring Ekaterina home from France. If he had to sneak around to be with her, it might as well be in the relative safety of St. Petersburg. She was given a palace a discreet distance from the royal family. She and Alexander had children. The gossip resumed, louder than ever. Alexander ignored it the way he had ignored the protests over the sale of Russian America.

The sale had not gone smoothly. Though the Tsar considered the contract binding from the moment it was signed, Seward still had to get the approval of the U.S. Senate to accept the treaty and then wrangle the money out of the House of Representatives to pay for it. This took another year and involved the chummy cajoling, clear-minded argument and occasional bribes that had made Seward such an asset for Lincoln.

Average Americans were in favor of acquiring more property, no matter how remote. But the purchase was a tough sell in Congress, made tougher by the impeachment of President Johnson.

Johnson's power began to unravel shortly after he approved the purchase of Alaska when he suspended Secretary of War Edwin Stanton in a spat over how to deal with the vanquished Southern states. Seward was a close friend of Stanton's but personally inclined to support Johnson's program of leniency. As a lawyer, he was also convinced that the President was in the right.

Congress disagreed. Johnson was impeached by the House early in 1868 and remained in office when the Senate voted 35 to 19 to convict him, one vote shy of the two-thirds needed to remove the President. Seward's own party held a strong grudge against him for siding with the President. Partly in retaliation, congressional Republicans held hearings about the shenanigans surrounding the deal to buy Russian America, not so much to undo the sale as to humiliate Seward. The investigation dragged on for months.

Despite the uncertainty of the impeachment crisis, the American takeover of Alaska continued on schedule. In October of 1867 General Jefferson Columbus Davis (not to be confused with the President of the Confederacy) arrived in New Archangel with U.S. troops for the transfer ceremony.

Officials and soldiers of both nations, Russian settlers and Tlingit residents gathered at Castle Hill, site of the governor's headquarters. Drums rolled and hats were removed as the Russian flag was lowered. But, to observers, it seemed that the flag did not want to come down. It snagged and refused to descend. A sailor climbed the pole to untangle the cloth and wound up dropping it. The banner fluttered toward the ground and landed on the upraised bayonets of the Russian honor guard. The wife of the last Russian governor, Princess Maria Maksutova, fainted.

Alaska, in the words of writer Bret Harte's poem "An Arctic Vision," now belonged to Uncle Sam.

In the same year another American writer, Samuel Clemens, better known as Mark Twain, met the Tsar in Yalta. The royal family was at the Black Sea for a summer holiday. Clemens was traveling with sightseers and officials on a trip that would become immortalized in his book "The Innocents Abroad."

The great humorist was impressed with both Alexander's majesty and his humility. The autocrat of the largest nation on Earth met his visitors in plain cotton clothes without jewelry or insignias. "No costume could be less ostentatious," Clemens wrote.

"He is very tall and spare, and a determined-looking man, though a very pleasant-looking one nevertheless. It is easy to see that he is kind and affectionate. There is something very noble in his expression when his cap is off. There is none of that cunning in his eye that all of us noticed in Louis Napoleon's."

The American tourists were amazed to hear everyone in the royal party speaking English. They were moved by the words with which Alexander greeted his guests. "There is character in them — Russian character — which is politeness itself, and the genuine article," Clemens observed.

He was particularly impressed when the Tsar and Tsarina, Maria Alexandrovna, personally walked the Americans through their mansion.

"As a general thing, we have been shown through palaces by some plush-legged filagreed flunkey or other, who charged a franc for it," Clemens recalled. "But after talking with the company half an hour, the Emperor of Russia and his family conducted us all through their mansion themselves. They made no charge. They seemed to take a real pleasure in it."

Clemens found the decor "rich but eminently home-like." He added, with a Twainian wink, that as soon as their guests had departed, the royals probably went through the palace and counted the silverware.

Twenty: Conquest and Discontent

While Alexander was divesting himself of property in the New World, he was acquiring more in Central Asia.

In 1865 General Mikhail Chernyayev was on the move in Uzbekistan. The Tsar gave direct orders that the heavily armed city of Tashkent should not be attacked until the Ministry of War approved a strategy.

Chernyayev was not a man to wait for bureaucrats to poke around on maps and theorize over a situation they knew nothing about. Though outnumbered 15 to one, his troops broke through the walls of Tashkent in a night attack. Two days later, the city was his. He had lost 25 men. The city's defenders had died by the thousands.

The victorious general let the Uzbeks know they'd been beaten. He rode through the city unarmed. He chatted with vendors in the bazaar and paid an honest price for what he bought. He stripped off his uniform and joined the town fathers in the steam bath where he listened to their concerns and promised to help. Within a week he was not just the conqueror of Tashkent but its beloved protector and unquestioned ruler.

Alexander was pleased, but also consternated. Clear orders had been disobeyed. Furthermore, the Tashkent victory was the result of a lot of luck, and one couldn't count on it happening twice. He recalled Chernyayev, gave him medals, showered bonuses on his troops and sent in a more regular sort of commander. Konstantin von Kaufman soon dashed whatever hopes the Uzbeks might have had for independence by bringing Russian settlers into the region.

Three years later von Kaufman took the city of Samarkand, south of Tashkent. The nearby nation of Kyrgyzstan, to the east, became Russian by treaty with China in 1876. Military pressure was kept up on Turkmenistan and Tajikistan, which would be conquered in 1881 and 1885, respectively.

Russia's military gains in Central Asia were part of what English-speaking historians like to call "The Great Game," a conflict between Russia, which was bent on expansion, and Great Britain, which was anxious to keep foreign fingers off its prize colony, India. It lasted for decades, a series of high-stakes chess moves in which the two largest modern armies in the area never once confronted each other.

Given the tension between Britain and Russia in Central Asia, the reception Alexander received when he visited London in 1874 was remarkably cordial.

His daughter Maria had married the second son of Queen Victoria, Prince Alfred, in January of that year, becoming the Duchess of Edinburgh and taking up residence in England. Neither Prime Minister Benjamin Disraeli nor the leader of the opposition, William Gladstone, was happy about having their foe in Asia treated as an honored guest at home. Both sides stressed that this was not an official state visit, only a father coming to see his daughter. Still, there were banquets, receptions and military reviews staged on his behalf and both Gladstone and Disraeli met with Alexander.

He seems not to have checked in with his old flame, Victoria. She had gone into seclusion after the death of her husband and was rarely seen in public. They would have had much to talk about. The Queen had survived two or three attempts on her own life. The Tsar had been shot at twice.

Disraeli found Alexander "gracious and graceful," but described his expression as sad. "Whether it is satiety, or the loneliness of despotism, or fear of a violent death, I know not," the Prime Minister wrote, "but it was a visage of, I should think, habitual mournfulness."

Alexander had worries from which Victoria was spared. In her prosperous country, public displeasure meant a change in government. In Russia, public displeasure could fracture the country and end his life. Despite the emancipation of the serfs, the powder keg had not been defused.

Alexander's liberal policies brought some benefits, but also allowed dissent to grow. On one hand he understood the need for educated people to have the freedom to turn their knowledge and energy into action on behalf of themselves, the state and civilization. On the other hand, if they used that freedom to call for the end of the monarchy, of religion, of business, the result could destroy the nation.

To stop any spark from igniting the powder, a network of spies kept tabs on everyone: the royal councilors and their mistresses, the workers in the factories, the clergy, military and students — especially the students, who were forever talking about the wrongs done to the lower classes.

Many of these students went into the countryside to work with and educate the peasants. They called themselves "narodniki," "crusaders for the people." But few of them knew how to plow, plant, fish or do any other kind of physical work. Even fewer liked being with the crude peasants, eating weak soup, sleeping in hay, seeing suffering and disease all around them.

A young noblewoman turned nurse, Vera Finger, described crowds of "dirty, emaciated" people filling her medical hut. "The diseases were all chronic," she wrote, "almost everyone had skin diseases." She was thrown into despair by the near-universal rheumatism, coughs, scabs, ulcers, syphilis and "unimaginable filth."

To give medicine in such poverty was both useless and hypocritical, she concluded. Finger changed her way of thinking. She decided that, instead of futile attempts to improve the condition of the poor with small acts of charity, the only remedy was to destroy the power structure that imposed the poverty in the first place. To destroy that structure, one needed to eliminate the Tsar.

It was an opinion shared by an increasing number of agitated young people. They met behind closed doors and earnestly discussed how that goal might be achieved.

The chief of the secret police, Peter Shuvalov, was excellent at his job, however. Troublemakers were sniffed out, apprehended and sent far away. The Tsar supported him. His brother Konstantin did not, but the survival of Russia was more important than family sentiment. When Shuvalov and Konstantin butted heads, as they often did, Alexander sided with his enforcer.

Politics, however, wasn't the only way a young person could get into trouble. In 1874, Konstantin's son Nikolai stole jewels from his mother to pay off his American mistress. Shuvalov solved the crime. Konstantin's influence — or interference — was extinguished, though too late to keep Alaska in the realm. Nikolai was sent away, presumably for medical treatment. But Alexander could not keep the truth hidden and the scandal diminished his prestige.

As part of the fallout, Shuvalov was removed as head of the secret police and made an ambassador. He was personally loyal to the Tsar, but during his tenure his department had become allied with parties that did not want Alexander's reforms to succeed. Although these conservatives considered radical students like Vera Finger to be a cancer on the state, they were open to at least one piece of the students' ideology — the proposition that the country might be better off with a different head of state.

Without Shuvalov's firm hand on the powerful agency, there was an inclination, ever so slight but dangerously real, for the secret police to put the good of the state, as they saw it, above the interests of the Tsar.

Twenty-one: The Road to Constantinople

Personal safety was not Alexander's main concern just then. He was planning what he envisioned as his greatest accomplishment. He would unify all people of Slavic origin under his rule and, at the same time, avenge the Crimean War.

Turkey was no stronger than it had been in the 1850s. France, which had brought about the war, was crippled by internal strife after the defeat of Napoleon III. Austria, also beaten by Bismarck, was in no position to intervene. The British were disinclined to wage another war if they could avoid it and distracted by opportunities to prosper while France was out of the picture. The Scandinavian nations were terrified by Prussia and Prussia was still trying to come to terms with German unification.

Alexander renounced the Treaty of Paris, which had ended the Crimean War on such distasteful terms. The other signatories protested but did not issue ultimatums. They doubted that his only purpose was altruistic: that is, to protect Slavic Christians in Ottoman territory. But they could not deny that those Slavs had legitimate grievances.

In 1875 the Christian majorities in the Balkan provinces of Bosnia and Herzegovina revolted. It was the first time a subject state had dared to declare its independence from Turkey. Serbia, Montenegro and Bulgaria eventually joined the uprising.

The response was brutal. Turkish soldiers burned villages, raped women, impaled children, slaughtered civilians and left their heads on pikes.

Reports of the atrocities inflamed the Russian public. Mobs demanded that the Tsar act, but Alexander's ministers argued that now was not the time. Only his usually docile son, the future Alexander III, was uncharacteristically vocal in urging his father to go to war.

Alexander informed Britain that he felt obliged to rescue his downtrodden brethren, but would only do so if it became necessary. Britain joined the chorus of nations publicly demanding that Turkey end the bloodshed. Privately, however, the British ambassador encouraged the Sultan to hang tough, assuring him that England would come to his aid if that proved to be necessary.

Impatient for war, Russian volunteers began pouring into the Balkans. Alexander brought brash General Chernyayev out of retirement and sent him to Serbia to form an army. The wild courage of the conqueror of Tashkent could be an advantage in the political fog that cloaked the Ottoman Empire's European possessions.

Political turmoil in Constantinople brought additional uncertainly; one Sultan was assassinated, another deposed within a matter of months. But the old general, the patriotic Serbs and the passionate Russian volunteers were no match for the Turkish army, which had many times more troops and the latest Krupp canons. The Serbs asked for a truce.

Suddenly every major power wanted to get in on negotiations. All loudly called for peace as they quietly prepared to slice up Turkey's European territory. Talks went on and the war went on and finally Alexander demanded a peace settlement for Montenegro. The Sultan rejected the demand and the fight was on.

Alexander declared war against the Ottoman Empire on April 12, 1877. He sent 250,000 troops across the Danube into Bulgaria. For the sake of comparison, the Allied forces that landed at Normandy on D-Day numbered 156,000.

In the knightly spirit of his warrior ancestors, the Tsar joined his men at the front.

The first detachments crossed Shipka Pass, the Balkan gate that would lead to Constantinople, but were thrown back. A few days later they took and held the pass, but could not advance.

The bulk of the Russian force was stalled with the powerful garrison at Plevna posing an imminent threat to its western flank. The commander, Osman Pasha, had 24,000 soldiers and extensive fortifications in place.

Alexander ordered Plevna attacked. Ten thousand Russians died in the first two assaults. Twelve thousand, along with 4,000 Romanian allies, died in a third attempt. Meanwhile, 25,000 Turks moved to take back Shipka Pass from 5,000 defenders. Russian and Bulgarian fighters held on for three days. They were out of ammunition and battling hand to hand when reinforcements arrived and turned the tide. The fresh troops had rushed 50 miles a day to get to the fight.

No sooner was the battle of Shipka Pass won than snow fell on the high country. Poorly supplied, their warm clothing stolen or sold off by corrupt officials, more Russians died from the cold than were killed by the Turks.

Freezing winds warned that winter was soon coming to the lowlands. Alexander would have to retreat, giving up the pass and Plevna, or risk one more assault on the fort. Until now his field commander had been his brother, Grand Duke Nikolai, whose wavering had caused the failure of the third assault. Alexander couldn't dismiss his brother, but he gave operational control to General Eduard Totleben, a military engineer who had taken part in the defense of Sevastopol.

Totleben saw that whatever losses Osman Pasha might be incurring, he could get supplies and reinforcements through a back route protected by a series of Turkish outposts. He ordered those outposts eliminated and the road closed.

After hard fighting, the Russians succeeded in creating a total blockade. The reinforcements that had previously crowded into Plevna meant more men to feed, and food was running out. The Turks attempted to evacuate the city but were forced back in. The final assault by 100,000 Russians brought the siege to an end.

Osman Pasha was brought before the Tsar, to whom he handed his sword. He expected it would be used on his own neck. But as he had with Shamil, Alexander handed it back as a sign of respect for his foe's courage. The Turk was stunned.

Snow fell heavily in the high passes between Plevna and southern Bulgaria, but Alexander was determined to build on his momentum. The Russians swept the Turks from the mountains and, on December 23, 1877, marched into Sofia, the capital of Bulgaria, without firing a shot.

The victors continued moving south through an eerie and empty landscape. The Muslim population had fled with all they could carry. Carts and wagons broken in the crush of the retreat were scattered along the way. So were the dead bodies of horses and people.

By early January Russian troops reached the village of San Stefano on the Aegean Sea. They were now less than 10 miles from Constantinople.

At this point England decided it had to step in. It sent warships into the Black Sea, prepared to confront the Russians should they get any closer. Soldiers and officers pleaded with Alexander to call the British bluff and let them take the great city. But his political ministers warned him that the country could not afford or prevail in another war against a united Europe.

The Russians sat down with the Ottoman representatives in San Stefano and dictated a peace settlement. The Turks gave to Russia Black Sea territory lost in the Crimean War and areas of the Caucasus. They agreed to pay an indemnity of 310 million rubles. Serbia, Montenegro and Romania were to become independent. Bulgaria would gain autonomy.

Britain and Austria did not like the treaty. Prussian Chancellor Bismarck suggested a conference to smooth out differences. Meeting with other world leaders in Berlin, the 80-year-old Russian foreign minister, Alexander Gorchakov, was clay in the hands of Bismarck and Disraeli who manipulated him into giving up many of Russia's gains. Only part of Bulgaria would remain free, fueling that nation's deep suspicion of foreign powers in the next 100 years. Austria, which had not taken part in the war, was given Bosnia and Herzegovina, a seemingly painless acquisition that would eventually set the stage for the First World War.

But the fight had not been fruitless. The Slavic states and Greece were now permanently free of Ottoman rule. And from their limited territory the Bulgarians would soon rise to push the Turks out for good.

Today a statue of Alexander II on horseback stands in the middle of Sofia. In Bulgaria, even more than in Finland or Russia itself, he is still known as the Liberator.

Twenty-two: Target of Terror

Tsar Alexander II with his "official" family, ca. 1870.
Standing left to right: Grand Duke Pavel, Grand Duke Sergei, Grand Duchess Maria,
Grand Duke Alexei, Tsarevich Alexander (later Tsar Alexander III), Grand Duke
Wladimir. Seated, left to right, Tsar Alexander II, Grand Duke Nicholas (later Tsar
Nicholas II), Grand Duchess Maria Fyodorovna, wife of Alexander III.

From Alexander's perspective, the outcome of the war with Turkey was a disaster. Gorchakov was humiliated. So were the Tsar, the Russian public and the army. It seemed that the gains achieved with the blood shed by thousands of brave soldiers had been carelessly lost at the negotiating table.

Everyone in Russia was angry and frightened. The fighting had put the government hundreds of millions of dollars in debt. The ruble plummeted in value and Russia's economy sank with it. The specter of a national famine loomed.

A small student movement, Land and Freedom, took root in this atmosphere. The party, if that word can be used, believed in the destruction of everything that constituted organized society. They called themselves nihilists and socialists. Today we would call them terrorists.

Attempts on the lives of Queen Victoria, Napoleon III and Alexander himself had previously been blamed on insane or disgruntled nationalists, the Irish and Poles or, in the case of Abraham Lincoln, a disgruntled Southern sympathizer.

But Russia's nihilists were a new breed, determined to use violence to destroy the government of their own country. Unlike impulsive madmen, they were calculating, coordinated and patient.

But they were also careless and left a broad path for the secret police to follow. In October of 1877 253 nihilists were arrested, of whom 160 were tried and convicted. The sweep took many of the movement's leaders off the street but left an uncertain number of adherents unidentified and looking for a chance to strike.

That chance came on January 28, 1878. General Fedor Trepov, the governor of St. Petersburg, was in his office when an ordinary-looking young woman, Vera Zasulich, came to him with a petition in one hand and a gun in the other. She fired, hitting Trepov in his buttocks.

The previous year, a trial of 193 people charged with various forms of sedition had led to convictions of 103. Most of the acquitted were exiled extra-judicially on Alexander's direct orders. But court proceedings were now open thanks to the Tsar's reforms. The arguments were reported in the newspapers, turning the lawyers into celebrities. Now every attorney in St. Petersburg wanted to defend Zasulich. It was a golden opportunity to become famous.

Zasulich admitted she intended to kill Trepov. But, to repeated ovations from the onlookers, her lawyer argued that an act of violence might be justified for the greater good.

The would-be assassin was acquitted and left the courtroom to a cheering crowd. Within minutes the cheering had turned into shouting and shooting. A policeman was killed.

Alexander was livid. Insofar as he was concerned, the law had not done its job. Judges, counselors and jurors had taken his well-intended reforms and made a mockery of them.

The foreign press exulted in Zasulich's acquittal. But other nations soon had reason to reconsider whether killing public figures was an appropriate way to make a political point. Similar attempts were made on the lives of the monarchs of Spain, Italy and Germany. In the decades that followed radicals driven by nihilist ideologies would kill an Austrian Empress, an Italian King, an American President and an Austrian Archduke, hurling the Western world into a previously unthinkable war.

The acquittal had serious repercussions in Russia. Police were shot in the streets. The governor of Kharkov and prosecutor of Kiev were killed. The head of the secret police, Nikolay Mezentsov, was eviscerated by a dagger-wielding "revolutionary socialist." Another assassination attempt was made on Mezentsov's replacement. "Evil is growing by the minute," wrote one official.

On April 2, 1879, Alexander was taking his usual morning walk on palace grounds in view of thongs who gathered on the street for a glimpse of him, when a well-dressed man with a military-style cap stepped from the crowd and pulled out a gun. The Tsar ran like a scared deer, leaping back and forth while four bullets zipped by him and another went through his coat. His bodyguards only caught the assailant after he stumbled. The shooter tried to swallow cyanide but his stomach was pumped and he remained alive. A noose reversed that condition shortly.

As some of its members became ever more violent, Land and Party members broke into two groups. One faction, born of the narodniki movement, favored education and working with the poor as the best way to change the country. The other, more radical party insisted on murdering those whom it held responsible for the state of the country, using terror to galvanize the nation into revolution.

The terrorists were in the minority, but their impact was enormous. They were ready not only to kill for their ideology but to die as well. They became their own secret society, eventually taking the name "People's Will." Their numbers included the one-time nurse to filthy peasants, Vera Finger, and another idealistic young woman, the daughter of the former Governor of St. Petersburg.

Her name was Sophia Perovskaya. She would succeed where all the hot-headed, loud-talking, cock-sure male revolutionaries of the movement failed.

Twenty-three: Dynamite Enters the Fray

Sophia Perovskaya, the mastermind of the assassination.

In addition to starry-eyed killers and twisted political theorists, People's Will included some well-trained scientific minds. They understood chemistry and mechanics. They knew of a new explosive called dynamite. They began talking about how it could be used to further the cause.

The group distributed proclamations and death sentences for officials before and after violent incidents. St. Petersburg was cloaked in fear of what the mysterious group that called itself the "Executive Committee" would do next.

Alexander declared martial law throughout the country. Battlefield generals took over as civilian governors. Trials again became closed. Increasing numbers of people were exiled and jailed. The mood of the nation was that of a state of siege.

Never before had a Tsar needed a bodyguard to go about in public. Now the royal family went nowhere without an armed escort. They were captives in their own capital. Alexander ordered the Tsarevich to relocate from his country estate to safer quarters inside the city. For the same reason, he moved Ekaterina and her children into the Winter Palace.

The presence of a royal mistress living on the floor above the Tsarina, who was ailing but still alive, scandalized the court. It was hardly the first time that a Tsar had kept a second family close at hand, but expectations had changed since the days of Peter the Great.

In the fall of 1879 Ekaterina traveled with Alexander to the Crimea. Tsarina Maria was on her own journey, to the resort of Sanremo, Italy, known for its doctors and salubrious climate. She expected to die there.

As the lovers enjoyed their time on the Black Sea, members of People's Will were busy making pounds of dangerously unstable dynamite, acquiring land near railroad tracks and gathering intelligence about how the Tsar would return to St. Petersburg. A coded message from a spy told them there would be two trains transporting the imperial party. The Tsar would be in the fourth car of the second train.

One of the nihilists was caught when he tried to move a heavy load of dynamite up the line from Odessa. A clever interrogator let him boast about the fine and noble intentions of People's Will. The interrogator acted like the ideas were an epiphany. Tell me more, he insisted. All Russia must know about this. You will lead mankind to a new dawn!

The vain nihilist talked and talked, gave names, addresses and details about 143 members of the the party. When he realized that he had been duped he hanged himself.

The arrests that followed didn't stop the plans of People's Will. On November 19, as the train rumbled from Moscow to St. Petersburg, a watchman counted the cars and, at the right moment, gave a signal. Dynamite planted under the tracks went off and blew the fourth car of the second train into the air.

The Tsar was not on board. A mechanical problem in Moscow had stopped the locomotive pulling the first train, which carried baggage and servants. Rather than wait, the Tsar had directed the train carrying him and Ekaterina to go ahead to St. Petersburg.

On his next trip to Moscow guards would stand on both sides of the track for hundreds of miles.

One of the train-bomb conspirators escaped to Paris and was granted protection by the French government. Alexander recalled his ambassador. He also brought the Tsarina back from the Mediterranean. Her condition had not improved. Reports of the new assassination attempt had shaken her nerves and made her health even worse.

As servants tucked her into a bed from which she would never arise, a bomb was being made within the very walls of the Winter Palace. A carpenter with ties to People's Will had earned the trust of the staff. He was given quarters two floors below the main dining room. He brought a trunk with him and slowly filled it with dynamite.

A lavish dinner was planned for 6 p.m. on February 5, 1880. The Tsar would be entertaining his brother-in-law. His sons would be with him. The carpenter set the fuse and walked to a tavern a safe distance away.

As it happened, a heavy snow slowed the arrival of the guests and delayed the entry of the dinner party. Alexander and his guests were just about to enter the dining room when they heard a thunderous sound and the floor rose under their feet like a wave.

The room was covered in plaster dust, as were the servants who remained standing at attention. Ash and smoke were so thick one could barely see the flames.

The nightmarish space was filled with the cries of guards who lived on the floor between the dining room and the place where the trunk of dynamite had been detonated. Some 50 men were dead or wounded.

People's Will issued a proclamation expressing sympathy for the deaths of "the wretched soldiers," but insisting that such collateral damage was "inevitable."

The bedridden Tsarina slept through it all. She slept through most things now, often hallucinating when conscious. She was aware of the second wife living one floor above her. But such was the lot of the wives of Tsars. Alexander still visited regularly and was solicitous about her needs. She still told him that she loved him. She probably meant it.

The Tsarevich Alexander, however, was devastated to learn of his father's infidelity. The heir was simple and soft-hearted. He didn't mind so much that his father was in love, but he couldn't stand to see how it pained his mother. Nonetheless, when the Tsar instructed him to take care of Ekaterina in the event that something should happen to him, the Tsarevich promised he would. And the father knew his sweet, gentle son would keep that promise.

In May of 1880 Maria Alexandrovna died in her sleep. Alexander wasted no time in marrying his morganatic wife and legitimizing her children. The court might still despise her, but now they would have to show respect. At least while the Tsar was around.

Twenty-four: The Hanky and the Bombs

*Alexander II and his "secret" wife, Ekaterina Dolgorukova
with their children George and Olga.*

By 1880 Alexander had grown convinced that repression was not
working. The terrorists had made two direct strikes on him that
he had escaped only by chance. Public opinion was sour. The harsh
measures imposed by the military governors had failed to end terror-
ism in any of the provinces — except one, Kharkov Oblast in Ukraine.

The Tsar's man in Kharkov was Mikhail Loris-Melikov, an
Armenian. He had proven exceptionally courageous and successful

during 30 years of duty in the Caucasus. He was a brilliant military leader, but he was also an intelligent administrator of civilian affairs, a skill almost totally lacking in the rest of the Russian government. He had the rare ability to be firm and still win the population to his side.

Following the bombing of the Winter Palace, Alexander created a new agency with full power to fight the terror. It was called the Supreme Administrative Commission for the War on Sedition. The Tsar named Loris-Melikov as the director.

Within days of receiving the appointment the new director was shot at. He tackled the gunman. The shooter was not a member of People's Will, only a young man inspired by the brazen deeds of the nihilists. He was hanged in short order, literally within hours.

Loris-Melikov had developed strong powers of observation on the battlefield. He wondered why, in a time of high alert, the guards had not noticed the suspicious, dishevelled man lurking nearby.

For that matter, how had the secret police missed the transport and placement of explosives under the train tracks and below the dining room of the Winter Palace? They had arrested and interrogated hundreds of people. They had gathered reams of information. What were they doing with it?

It may have occurred to Loris-Melikov, as it has to historians of a later generation, that the secret police were intentionally ignoring leads and information that could end the terror threat. This theory implies that people in the Third Department secretly hoped the overly-sensitive Tsar would be replaced by a ruler with more conservative views. The Tsarevich, for instance.

Alexander asked Loris-Melikov to prepare a report on how the turmoil could be put to an end. Loris-Melikov's proposals included disbanding the Third Department, restoring earlier reforms, giving greater freedom to the press, making it easier to travel, enacting improvements in education and giving rights to non-Orthodox religious groups. The Tsar agreed.

University students, who had been writhing with rebellion over restrictions imposed on them, suddenly found they no longer had anything to rebel against. The press swung back into the Tsar's camp; they respected Loris-Melikov because he respected them and told the truth about what was possible.

Calm set in almost immediately. The attacks stopped.

In August Alexander dissolved the Supreme Commission. Its goals had been achieved. Or so it seemed.

He made Loris-Melikov Minister of the Interior and let him retain the exceptional powers he had exercised as the commission's director. Together they began work on the Tsar's most monumental project yet — the writing of a constitution.

The Tsar had been moving in the direction of allowing elected officials to take part in the creation of laws, giving up a large portion of his power. It would be the first time that a Russian ruler allowed any kind of popular representation in government. He had worked on the idea with his brother Konstantin, but it was put on hold following the bombing of the Winter Palace. Now, with peace in the realm, he was ready to act.

Loris-Melikov prepared a draft constitution in January of 1881. The Tsar found it met his expectations. On February 17 he gave orders to proceed with the plan at an early date.

The proposed constitution was still, officially, a state secret. But rumors about it gained traction after the 25th anniversary of the Emancipation Manifesto. Conservatives were frustrated, liberals giddy.

People's Will panicked. If the constitution were to come to pass, their terrorist acts would not be seen as targeting an evil dictator, but as assaults on the consensus of the public. They knew time was running short and redoubled their efforts. It may have caused them to become careless.

In preparing to do away with the Third Department, Loris-Melikov set up his own police force, more professional than the sloppy secret police but with parallel powers. They quickly picked up one member of the organized nihilist movement after another by simply following clues the old agency had ignored or failed to act upon. They caught a mole who had been working inside the Third Department and passing information along to the nihilists for two years.

By March of 1880 the leadership of People's Will, including men who had taken part in several killings, were under arrest. Sixteen went on trial in October. Five were sentenced to death. Alexander pardoned three.

The arrests reduced People's Will to a fugitive remnant. They included Nikolai Kibalchich, the explosives genius, and Sophia Perovskaya.

The scare engendered by so many attempts on his life had caused Alexander to vary his schedule and his routes. But one long-established tradition continued. Every Sunday he attended the changing of the guard and military parade at the Mikhailovsky Manège, a gigantic riding academy in the center of town. Crowds always lined the streets to see him pass.

There were only two routes to and from the manège. The remaining nihilists devised plans to get bombs to either site and prepared to strike on Sunday, March 1, 1881. But on February 27 they had a serious setback when the remaining top three leaders were arrested by Loris-Melikov's police.

The handful of radicals who remained met in disarray. It was Saturday and none of the bombs was ready. They would have to postpone the deed. But each day's delay made it ever more possible that they, too, would be found out.

As the group quarreled and vacillated, Sophia Perovskaya took the floor. In fiery language she put steel into the quavering men. They must kill the Tsar for the revolution to begin, she said. And they must do so within 24 hours, no matter what.

The inspired group went to work with a will. By the next morning the bombs were ready. A large one had been placed under Malaya Sadovaya Street through a tunnel the conspirators had dug from a nearby building. Four smaller portable bombs were in the hands of men who would throw them if something went wrong with the tunnel dynamite. In the event that the route switched to the Catherine Canal, they could quickly reposition themselves and toss the bombs there.

The Tsar had a lovely morning. Loris-Melikov brought him the final announcement regarding the new constitution and Alexander ordered a meeting of ministers to be held in three days. The constitution would be presented and formally promulgated at that time. The date — and his name — would be remembered forever.

As he prepared to leave for the Mikhailovsky Manège, he stopped in Ekaterina's room to say good-bye. She had a premonition and, with tears in her eyes, begged him not to go. Alexander dismissed her worries and, according to his doctor's recollection, calmed her by making love to her on a table in the room. Then he left to attend the ceremony and visit a relative along the way.

Alexander traveled in the bullet-proof carriage given to him by Napoleon III. Seven Cossack guards accompanied him. The chief of police and captain of the Tsar's guards followed in two sleds.

The review went well. The Tsar was pleased. He returned to his carriage and instructed the driver to return to the Winter Palace via the Catherine Canal.

From a vantage point where she could see the action in several directions, Perovskaya saw the guards on Malaya Sadovaya Street depart and realized the tunnel explosion plan would not work. She raised her handkerchief to her face and blew her nose.

That was the signal to the men carrying bombs to move to the canal.

As Alexander's party came around the corner a young man in a black coat carrying a white package stepped forward and hurled the package at the carriage. The explosion knocked Cossacks off their horses.

The carriage was surrounded by smoke, but only the back was damaged. The Tsar got out, unharmed, and watched his men catch the assailant.

On the street one Cossack was dead. Another was wounded. A boy lay in the snow screaming and dying.

The bomb thrower could be heard calling to someone in the crowd. Alexander's guards grasped that there was another potential assassin, perhaps more than one, still in the area. They pleaded with the Tsar to get back in the carriage, or get out of the vicinity in one of the sleds.

Instead he walked to where the bomb thrower was held, shook his finger at him and paced along the canal to take a close look at where the bomb had gone off.

Another man waited for him to come close then threw the second bomb at his feet. Twenty people were brought down by the explosion, burned, deafened, bleeding and dying.

The assassination of Alexander II, newspaper illustration.

Among those fatally wounded was the 62-year old Tsar. His legs had been smashed. Blood streamed from him.

There was a military hospital close at hand. Had he been taken there without delay, the bleeding might have been stopped in time to save his life.

Instead, with his consciousness fading, he gave his final command. "Take me home. To the Palace. There to die."

Twenty-five: Aftermath and Speculation

The execution of the conspirators, London Times illustration.

They brought Alexander back to the Winter Palace on a stretcher in an open sled. They ripped out narrow doorjambs to get him to his study. In that room, surrounded by his family, he breathed his last.

All were crying, some hysterically, others sniffing in futile attempts to keep back tears. One by one the moist eyes turned toward the heir, the slow, weak-minded, tender-hearted, overgrown boy who was now Alexander III.

They hardly recognized him. The boy had transformed into a bear. There was a set to his jaw, an icy gleam in his eye. In an instant everyone realized that the new Tsar would rule with the iron fist of his grandfather, with a ruthlessness that his father never managed to have the stomach for.

There would be no constitution. The reforms of courts and press would be rolled back. All power would be centralized at the Tsar's desk. All decisions would flow from his inkwell. No progressive changes would be considered, even when the status quo meant suffering for millions.

The feared famines would come. The economy would languish. Persecution of Jews and oppression of vassal states would be resurrected. The military would grow so calcified that, within 25 years, it was smashed and humiliated by the small but efficient armed forces of little Japan.

The conspirators were hanged on April 3, 1881, five together at the same time. The bomb-makers, the bomb-throwers and Sophia Perovskaya.

The tough policies of Alexander III would bring a semblance of peace to the country for a while. But discontent continued to build and eventually erupted in a revolution that brought the murder of his heir, Tsar Nicholas II, along with his whole family, a revolution that culminated in a long reign of terror that the world will shudder to recall for centuries to come.

Loris-Melikov resigned and retired to Nice. Nice was also where Ekaterina and her children went to live. She died there in 1922. Her love affair with Alexander was made into a French movie with Danielle Darrieux in 1938 and another in Germany, with Romy Schneider, in 1959 — the same year that the former Russian America became America's 49th state.

At the spot where the bombs went off, Alexander III ordered the construction of a magnificent church, one of the most awe-inspiring and beautiful houses of worship in the world. It is known as the Temple on Spilled Blood.

The church is a must-see for every tourist who comes to St. Petersburg. So is the Cathedral of Saints Peter and Paul. Nearly all of Russia's Tsars from Peter the Great to Nicholas II are buried here, each in an identical white marble sarcophagus. But visitors will notice two of the tombs are different. A pink rhodonite monument contains the body of Tsarina Maria Alexandrovna.

Next to it, in similarly-carved gray-green jasper, lies Alexander the Liberator.

A historian is not an author, one who creates something new. He is only a writer who, if he does his job well, reports what others have already recorded. But when the writing is done, he sometimes reflects on how history might have been different had a few actions been taken or avoided or transpired at a time other than when they did — sometimes a matter of minutes or seconds.

What if Alexander had not been inclined to sell Russian America? The transaction was not preordained, according to Chevigny. "A nation having small desire to sell did so to a nation that was not eager to buy," he writes. Each side was inexplicably motivated by "the belief they would please the other."

Most Russians left Alaska after the transfer. Alaskan historian Lydia Black laments that the creoles, the backbone of Russian America, were relegated to second class status by the English-speaking newcomers. In the dozen years that followed the purchase the non-Native ethnic Russian population would almost disappear and no new settlements would be started.

Not until 1880, when gold was discovered in the vicinity of present day Juneau, did new migrants begin to drift north and stay.

How would a Russian-speaking, Russia-ruled Alaska have fared during the Russo-Japanese War? After the Communist Revolution? How would it have affected the alliance between the U.S. and the Soviet Union in World War II?

What if Alexander III had continued the policies of his father and enacted the constitution? Would a Russian form of responsible liberty have taken root? Would we even know the names of Lenin or Stalin today?

And, for the connoisseurs of conjecture, consider this: Among the conspirators was the bomb-maker, Kibalchich. As he was awaiting execution he frantically made notes and diagrams for a device that would fly through the air. You must get these papers to the scientists, he told his attorney. It will benefit the country and mankind.

But the papers were not shown to anyone and only discovered a quarter of a century later. They were plans for a rocket. The design doesn't look practical, but what if Alexander III had been notified

Nikolai Kibalchich, the explosives genius who made the bomb that killed Tsar Alexander II.

of it by a knowledgeable party and suspended Kibalchich's punishment so that he could refine his plans? Even with the manufacturing technology of the 1880s, it might have given Russia a weapon no one else had or could imagine, a superweapon that could have conquered Europe and China.

This scenario may sound like science fiction. And yet it is a fact of astronomy that a crater on the moon is named for Nikolai Kibalchich. In 1959 the Russian space probe Luna 3 took the first photographs of the far side of the moon and Soviet officials named the craters and other features. To them Kibalchich was both a pioneer of science and a revolutionary martyr.

Such speculations are idle, but history writers are susceptible to them.

We are also prone to unintentionally developing a certain affection for the people we write about, whose deeds and thoughts we try to understand. You cannot study a saint without discovering his flaws. You cannot study a psychopath without getting a glimpse of how he justified his actions, why he thought he was doing the right thing. We are all human.

The assessment of Sam Clemens — Mark Twain — is instructive. Twain was never shy about identifying fraud and inhumanity wherever he saw it, whether among royalty, religious, radicals, riffraff or "plush-legged filigreed flunkeys." He knew the Tsar was an absolute dictator and he understood, with greater clarity than a modern American can, what that meant.

Yet in his brief meeting with Alexander II, Mark Twain saw kindness, concern for his family, friendliness and honesty. He found himself liking his host.

"If I could have stolen his coat, I would have," he wrote. "When I meet a man like that I want something to remember him by."

The choices Alexander made for right or wrong are still debated among Russians. He remains famous there. Yet his name and legacy are hardly known in America, even in Alaska, which was once part of his realm.

And so, reader, I present this book. To give you something to remember him by.

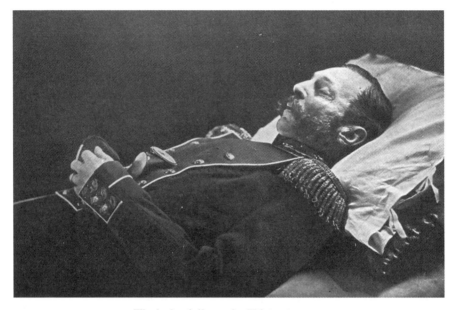

The body of Alexander II lying in state.

Bibliography

Atiya, Jeremy *The Great Land: How Western America Nearly Became a Russian Possession*. Oxford: Parker Press, 2008

Black, Lydia T. *Russians in Alaska, 1732-1867*. Fairbanks: University of Alaska Press, 2004

Chevigny, Hector *Russian America: The Great Alaskan Venture, 1741-1867*. New York: Viking Press, 1965

Jaimoukha, Amjad *The Circassians, A Handbook*. New York: Palgrave, 2001

Kaplan, Robert D. *The Revenge of Geography*. New York: Random House, 2012

Naske, Claus-M. and Slotnick, Herman E. *Alaska: A History*. Norman: University of Oklahoma Press, 2014

Sipes, Ernest *Into the Savage Land: The Alaskan Journal of Edward Adams*. Surrey, British Columbia: Hancock House, 2007

Steller, Georg (trans. Engel, Margritt and Williams, Karen) *Steller's History of Kamchatka*. Fairbanks, University of Alaska Press, 2003

Radzinsky, Edvard *Alexander II: The Last Great Tsar*. New York: Free Press, 2005

Seward, Frederick *William Seward at Washington as Senator and Secretary of State: A Memoire of His Life, with Selections from His Letters, 1861- 1872*. New York: Derby and Miller, 1891

Von Lowenstern, Hermann Ludwig (trans. Moessner, Victoria Joan) *The First Russian Voyage around the World*. Fairbanks, University of Alaska Press, 2003

Walsh, Stephan *Musorgsky and His Circle: A Russian Musical Adventure*. New York: Alfred A. Knopf, 2013

About the Author

Photo by Erik Hill

A native of Pampa, Texas, Michael Dunham lived as a small child in the western Alaska Native village of Quinhagak in the 1950s where he saw elders said to have been born when the territory was part of the Russian Empire. He is a graduate of Anchorage West High School.

After Alaska became a state, he studied history at the University of Washington in Seattle. He graduated Summa Cum Laude from the University of St. Thomas in Houston, Texas. Over the past 50 years he has worked in a variety of jobs at Alaska radio stations and as an editor, reporter and arts critic at the ***Anchorage Times***, ***Anchorage Daily News*** and ***Alaska Dispatch News***.

Dunham is the author of several entries in *"**Frommer's Guide to Alaska**"* and has been a contributor to the BBC, ***Opera***, ***Orion*** and ***Reason*** magazines. He is the co-editor of Osahito Miyaoka's *"**A Grammar of Central Yupik.**"* Contact him at Box 220152, Anchorage, AK 99522.